THE GENIUS O

GW00360295

E

The Genius of Irish Prose

Edited by

Augustine Martin

The Thomas Davis Lecture Series
General Editor: Michael Littleton

Published in collaboration with
Radio Telefís Éireann
by
THE MERCIER PRESS
DUBLIN and CORK

The Mercier Press Limited
4 Bridge Street, Cork
24 Lower Abbey Street, Dublin 1

The Genius of Irish Prose
First Published 1985

The Genius of Irish prose
    1. English literature — Irish authors —
History and criticism
    I. Martin, Augustine II. Radio Telefis Eireann
820.9'9415   PR8750

ISBN 0-85342-728-3

Printed by Litho Press Co. Ltd., Midleton, Co. Cork

The Thomas Davis Lectures
General Editor: Michael Littleton
Every autumn, winter and spring since September 1953, Radio Telefis
Éireann has been broadcasting half-hour lectures, named in honour of
Thomas Davis. Inspired by one of his famous sayings, 'Educate that you
may be free', the aim of these lectures has been to provide in popular form
what is best in Irish scholarship and the sciences.

    Most of the lectures have been in series; many have been single broadcasts;
some have been in English; some in Irish. In the time that has passed since
they were initiated the lectures have dealt with many aspects and with many
centuries of Irish social life, history, science and literature. The lecturers,
distinguished for their special learning at home and abroad, have been drawn
from many nations but mainly from Ireland.

Contents

Introduction

The fourteen lectures that comprise this book attempt to define and evaluate that great body of imaginative prose writing that has come out of Ireland in this century. Comprehensiveness was impossible within the space available, but a determined attempt has been made to deal with what is genuinely significant in the various *genres* while pointing towards those areas of achievement or promise which were impossible to accommodate within the central emphasis of each chapter. Each contributor is an expert within his field, but even the most authoritative judgments are to some degree subjective, especially in the highly subjective regions of literature. The book offers itself in terms of lively and informed opinion, rather than in any spirit of dogma. If the views and discriminations offered prove in some cases controversial so much the better. The object of all good criticism is to stimulate, even provoke discussion of what the creative artist has engendered.

In contacting the thirteen contributors and proposing to each his topic I became aware that some of my categories seemed a little puzzling if not positively eccentric. Derry Jeffares first talked and then wrote himself into his sense of a species called 'the realist novel', and Seán McMahon raised as many knotty points over the telephone before settling down to his brief. In fact it was the existence of a vigorous and special Irish manifestation of the novel, a form markedly unrealistic, that forced the distinction upon me. To make the point I had to take this narrative form upon myself, calling it 'fable and fantasy' and declaring all the rest 'realist'. I don't think this distinction would have been necessary in most other national traditions; the word 'novel' would not have required the word 'realist' to clinch its identity.

The reasons for this are to be found in social history, religion, folklore, the development of literature itself. It would be hard to imagine the procession of Yeats, Stephens, Joyce, Flann O'Brien, Mervyn Wall, taking its way through British or American prose narrative. Similarly the course of realist fiction constantly takes its force, colour and direction from political and societal tendencies and events unique to Ireland. The body of material was too large for a single lecture – even with John Cronin's retrospect on the nineteenth century – and the natural place of the *caesura* seemed the Second World War.

The only other *genre* requiring a joint treatment was the short story in which Ireland claims special status for the number of good writers the form has attracted and the range of formal and thematic experiment and innovation it has provoked. It is hard to say whether Colbert Kearney or John Jordan had the more challenging task; the one defining the achievement of the great established figures from Joyce and Moore to Mary Lavin, the other, himself a fine short story writer, making his discriminations among that flowering of talent in the field since the mid-forties. It is for the individual reader to speculate as to whether Frank O'Connor's famous distinction still holds: does the novel by nature address itself to the rhythms of an established social life? is the short story essentially the literature of 'lonely men', of the submerged population group? Has each something different to communicate about life as it is lived in contemporary Ireland?

The categories are still under fire as Benedict Kiely begins by suggesting, incontrovertibly, that all novels are in a sense historical novels, though he has no difficulty in settling upon the few genuine masterpieces we have produced in this *genre*. And the distinction between 'autobiography' and 'autobiographical fiction' helps merely to alert us to what great originality Irish writers have brought to both these literary modes.

Terence Brown notes how 'through autobiography after autobiography the main and lesser personages of the period would weave their way like characters in a never-ending fictional saga. . . Moore, Yeats, Synge, O'Casey, Edward Martyn, Gogarty, George Russell, Hyde, Lady Gregory, Maud Gonne. . .' But though George Moore's trilogy, *Ave, Salve, Vale,* has the sparkle, inventiveness, even the mendacity of fiction, it is a totally different literary animal from Joyce's great *bildungsroman, A Portrait of the Artist as a Young Man* or Francis Stuart's *Black List, Section H.* Thomas Kilroy's handling of the latter makes it clear that the growth novel had unique opportunities in a country so small, an ethos so stern and uniform, and a society so intimate as Ireland offered the writer of fiction. These same qualities of space and intimacy were the very conditions that made the straight, or crooked, autobiography thrive, especially if, like Moore and O'Casey, the author could direct his fire from the comparative safety of exile.

Two other forms of imaginative prose remained to be charted on this literary landscape. Maurice Harmon addresses himself to that less subjective, more scholarly, but no less imaginative *genre,* the literary autobiography, a form that is becoming so increasingly prominent in our time that it is often felt to be replacing the novel. And Proinsias Ó Conluain takes on a manifestation of Irish culture that had its powerful beginnings in the writers of the Great Blasket, Thomás Ó Croimhthain, Muiris Ó Súileabháin and Peig Sayers and continues in the work of Breandán Ó hEithir and Donall Mac Amhlaigh – that prose work in Irish whose merit and relevance has demanded translation into English for a readership unable to cope with it in its original.

Three major Irish writers, Moore, Joyce, and Beckett, can be said to partake in and transcend almost every mode and *genre* of literary creation I have been rehearsing – novel, short story, fable and fantasy, *bildungsroman.* Richard Cave, Denis Donoghue and Declan Kiberd deal with this giant triumvirate not according to any prescriptive formula but in terms of a free and personal response to their achievement as writers. These three great citizens of the world of letters remain incorrigibly Irish. Like the columns of a suspension bridge they tower above the fluent traffic of contemporary Irish writing, while at the same time giving it inspiration, direction and support.

Augustine Martin
1984

1. The Nineteenth Century: A Retrospect

John Cronin

The nineteenth century in Ireland was a troublesome time in which to be alive and it proved a vastly difficult period for writers to write about. Outbursts of agrarian violence were common, often initiated by bands of desperate terrorists with names such as Whiteboys, Rockites, Shanavests and so on. There were numerous famines in the earlier part of the century, culminating in the horror of the Great Hunger of 1845. There were two notably unsuccessful insurrections, in 1848 and 1867, and the close of the century witnessed a grim struggle for the repossession of the land by the people. In addition to all this, the Irish language was rapidly declining and English was coming to the fore as the common language of the great mass of the people. Thus, the writers of the period had to carry out their task in an emergent idiom and in an atmosphere compounded of various kinds of uncertainty and social unrest. The clear social patterns which provided such stability for their English counterparts were not available to them. Nor was there any large reading public in Ireland itself, so that the Irish writers had to devise an appropriate idiom or set of idioms and aim their work mainly at a largely alien and often unsympathetic audience in England, from whom they could expect little in the way of genuine understanding of local history or conditions. Accordingly, it will be clear that attempting a retrospective survey of the fiction of the nineteenth century in Ireland will call for an energetic exercise of the historical imagination and a certain amount of critical sympathy of a special kind. If we begin by recognising that the period produced a great many genuinely talented novelists but remarkably few great novels, we shall at least have enunciated the apparent contradiction which we shall have to resolve. Such a paradoxical formulation clearly implies the existence in the period of special circumstances of a peculiarly inhibiting nature, which made the task of the writers a particularly difficult one.

The century opens with the Act of Union, which deprived Ireland of its parliament and robbed Dublin of the brief metropolitan glory which it had enjoyed during the closing decades of the eighteenth century. Pitt had forced the Union through by means of wholesale bribery and corruption and had worked to convince the Catholics that their political prospects would be more favourable under a Westminster administration than under an Irish Protestant parliament in Dublin. They were to learn how mistaken this view was as Relief Act after Relief Act was voted down in London and the struggle for Catholic Emancipation ground on grimly for another thirty years, firstly under Grattan and later under O'Connell. This was a dark period during which, according to the historian, Edmund Curtis, only four or five years were of normal civil government.[1] The most important writer at work in Ireland at this time was Maria Edgeworth, whose four Irish novels, *Castle Rackrent, Ennui, The Absentee* and *Ormond,* appeared between 1800 and 1817. This talented woman had created in *Castle Rackrent* one of the most memorably astute and ironic insights into her own class of declining gentry and, in her other Irish novels, had surveyed the Irish society of her time perceptively, if somewhat didactically. She had also written novels with English settings as well as works of an educational nature and had acquired a European reputation, being fêted in the literary salons of Paris when she travelled to France with her father. She was to find, however, that the Ireland of her day was becoming more and more unmanageable as a basis for her fiction. In 1834 she was to write a revealing letter to a relative, in which she confessed that she could no longer write about the troubled country of her adoption: 'It is impossible to draw Ireland as she now is in a book of fiction – the realities are too strong, party passions too violent, to bear to see, or care to look at their faces in the looking glass. The people would only break the glass, and curse the fool who held the mirror up to nature – distorted nature, in a fever. We are in too perilous a case to laugh, humour would be out of season, worse than bad taste.'[2] And so, this most gifted of the early novelists fell silent on the subject of Ireland, though she was to continue to publish other works until as late as 1848.

Maria Edgeworth had been, in the most precise sense of the term, an Anglo–Irishwoman, born in England and educated there until her teens, then spending the rest of her long life at the family estate at Edgeworthstown. The grim Ireland which gradually defeated her fictionally found expression in the works of three gifted, native Irish writers all born at about the same time, William Carleton (b. 1794), John Banim (b. 1798) and Gerald Griffin (b. 1803). These three were all coming to maturity in the twenties and thirties of the century and it is in their novels and stories that we find pictured the violent and confused Ireland of the period between the Union and the Great Famine. Griffin and Banim both died comparatively young, just before the Famine broke out, while Carleton was to live on until 1869. It is in the works of these three in particular that we can witness the peculiar creative tensions to which reference was made at the beginning. They confronted in their various ways crippling problems concerning the troublesome material of their fiction as well as its idiom and audience. On the other hand, it was in their favour that they found themselves writing regional novels and stories at a time when the appetite of English readers for that sort of fare had been whetted by the Romantic poets and the novels of Sir Walter Scott. A writer in the *Edinburgh Review* in 1826, discussing Irish novels, conveys clearly the English public's complete ignorance of Ireland, an ignorance which made them entirely willing to welcome it as a fictional territory in which almost anything might be expected to happen: 'The advantage of being a *terra incognita,* at least to English statesmen, Ireland has, till lately, possessed almost as fully as the interior of Africa. Even at present, a writer who lays the scene of his story. . . in the kingdom of Connemara, is assuredly as safe there from topographical criticism as he would be from the King's writ, and may describe away with as little fear of surveillance or detection as if he were writing about Fatteconda or Timbucktoo.'[3]

John Banim, with the able assistance of his brother, Michael, was the first to exploit the vogue for melodramatic regional fiction which depicted violent events set in exotic locations. In 1825, the Banims had a success with the first volume of their *Tales by the O'Hara Family*, the second series of which appeared in the following year. Gerald Griffin followed suit in 1827 with a book of regional short stories called *Holland-Tide*. The attractions of such works for the English reader are obvious. They depict an unfamiliar landscape, a romantically wild place where almost any exciting event may occur. They recount unusual local customs, intriguing local characters, country craftsmen, rural beliefs and superstitions, and they present all this in a version of the English language which has the charm of being filtered through a strange neighbour tongue which imparts to the speech of the characters an engaging vividness and a curious kind of attraction. Throw over the lot a melodramatic love story or terrorist plot (or both) and the resultant mixture proved very much to the taste of English readers of the 1820s and 1830s. Side by side with this fictional inclination went a taste for historical novels and John Banim obliged in 1826 with his ambitious imitation of Scott in *The Boyne Water*. Griffin spent several years laboriously researching the Viking period in Ireland and produced his very lengthy and rather slow-moving novel, *The Invasion*, in 1832. In a note which he appended to the double volume which he published late in 1829, *The Rivals and Tracy's Ambition*, Griffin made an interesting distinction between his own work and that of the Banims. He first describes what he saw as the fictional achievement of the Kilkenny brothers: 'The authors who write under the assumed name of the "O'Hara Family" were the first who painted the Irish peasant sternly from the life: they placed him before the world in all his ragged energy and cloudy loftiness of spirit, they painted him as he is, goaded by the sense of national and personal wrong and venting his long pent up agony in the savage cruelty of his actions, in the powerful idiomatic eloquence of his language, in the wild truth and unregulated generosity of his sentiments, in the scalding vehemence of his reproaches and biting satire of his jests.'[4]

His own work Griffin sees as being of a gentler sort: 'We have endeavoured in most instances, where pictures of Irish cottage life have been introduced, to furnish a softening corollary to the more exciting moral chronicles of our predecessors, to bring forward the sorrows and affections more frequently than the violent and fearful passions of the people.'⁵

What this means in practice is that, while the Banims specialised in a particularly horrific kind of melodramatic tale such as *Crohoore of the Bill-Hook,* Griffin was at his happiest with scenes of a milder, more domestic nature. Both writers, though, had a fondness for the depiction of romantic, wild scenery, lonely glens, rushing waterfalls, steep and gloomy mountains, lofty cliffs and stormy seascapes. Griffin's best-known novel, *The Collegians,* published in 1829, is rich in this sort of scenic variety, with some of its more vivid episodes such as the fateful encounter between the hero, Hardress Cregan and his villainous servant, Danny Mann, being played out in appropriately Gothic surroundings.

William Carleton, though he wrote upwards of a dozen novels in his long career, achieved what most critics would account his most memorable fictional performance in the early 1830s with the publication of the two series of his *Traits and Stories of the Irish Peasantry.* In these, drawing on his vivid memories of his childhood in County Tyrone, he presents with Chaucerian largesse a great gallery of lively country characters, pouring forth a memorable series of portraits of hedge-schoolmasters, faction fighters, dancing masters, 'poor scholars', country fiddlers, and setting the country folk of his youth to their favourite activities at fairs and weddings, at wakes and pilgrimages. In celebrated stories like the horrific *Wildgoose Lodge* he depicted also the darker aspects of the brutal violence of the times. The serious artistic defects which beset his novels – his tendency to lapse into digressions of all sorts, his inability to organise a lengthy plot – these matter less in the short stories, where his delight in all kinds of human idiosyncrasy and his joy in verbal comedy combine to produce such memorable figures as Denis O'Shaughnessy on his talkative way to Maynooth or the wondrous advertisement composed by the inhabitants of the village of Findramore in their desperate search for a schoolmaster. Carleton's potent stew of rich comedy and verbal pyrotechnics looks forward to the later achievements of writers such as James Stephens, James Joyce, Flann O'Brien and the early Beckett.

It is in the works of these native novelists, then, that we can find depicted for us the forgotten world of the ordinary Irish people whose lives lie on the other side of that appalling mid-century hiatus in the national life known as the Great Hunger. In the fictions of the Banims, Griffin and Carleton, the people of the small towns and country places of Ireland live again the life of the period between the Union and the Great Famine. The work of these writers was, inevitably, an uneasy amalgam of the artistic and the socially purposeful. Though their stories and novels may differ from one another in various ways, emphasising different aspects of the Irish character and highlighting varying aspects of Ireland's history, all have one central purpose in common. They are all passionately devoted to a specific missionary purpose, that of convincing the English public of the essential decency of the ordinary Irish people. This is what causes the American novelist and critic, Thomas Flanagan, to characterise their fiction as being 'a kind of advocacy before the bar of English public opinion'.[6] Worthy as the purpose was, it was artistically damaging. Again and again, the fiction will be blemished by lengthy explanatory asides of an economic or political nature, directed at the English reader in an understandable, if regrettable attempt to help him to get to know the strange occupants of the sister island, and to understand the tangled history which has made them what they are. The standard novelistic stratagem which derived directly from this urge to explain and justify the Irish people to the English is the introduction into many of the novels and stories of the visiting Englishman, the 'stranger in Ireland', the nineteenth century literary tourist who wanders through Irish fiction from the very beginning, admiring the scenery and learning the charms and oddities of the Irish in their native habitat. From Edgeworth's Lord Colambre in *The Absentee* to Griffin's Captain Gibson in *The Collegians*, to the accident-prone Leigh Kelway in Somerville and Ross's short story, *Lisheen Races Second Hand*, the Irish fiction of the nineteenth century, in its eagerness to elucidate and justify, employs a whole series of visiting go-betweens who are made to run a gamut of experiences which range from mild enlightenment to hilarious discomfiture. If one were to search for a comparable fictional

tactic in modern times, one might find something roughly
similar in the passion of journalistic explication which has
been operating in regard to the Ulster 'Troubles' of the last
decade and a half. This has, to some extent, spilt over into the
fiction of this period also since, even today, writers cannot
assume any familiarity on the part of a largely indifferent
British public with the identities and origins of local political
groupings and organisations. It is with a sad sense of *deja-vu*
that one sees the Irish novel equip itself once again with visiting
English politicians, built-in explanations and even,
sometimes, elaborate afternotes.

As Thomas Flanagan indicates, the well-meant intrusion
into the fiction of the early 1800s of this kind of earnest
explication was often intended to persuade the English readers
to view the events of Ireland as tragic ones. He is surely right
when he suggests that the writers almost certainly failed in
this purpose. The English reading public has always been more
willing to see Irish events as comic, and this may account for
the popularity of such writers as Charles Lever, Samuel Lover
and Somerville and Ross and for the attendant fact that the
more serious works of such writers tend to be ignored in
favour of their lighter fictions. Thus, for example, Lever's
earlier works, which he undertook in a spirit of light-hearted
amateurism, tend to be preferred to his later, more solid
novels, and the 'R.M.' stories of Somerville and Ross earned
them more money and popularity than their splendid novel,
The Real Charlotte. Samuel Lover's comic novel, *Handy Andy,*
published in 1842, enjoyed huge popularity and has remained
almost constantly in print. It has enraged many Irish critics
who have seen its central portrait of Andy Rooney, the Irish
servant with a talent for farcical disaster and a highly
improbable way with the the English language, as the very
quintessence of stage-Irishry. The novel is, in fact, more
interesting as a demonstration, if such were needed, of the
sheer impossibility of writing a comic novel about the chaotic
and doomed Ireland of the mid-century. In a period when
tragic writing often toppled over into a lurid melodrama it
was, perhaps, inevitable, that attempts at comedy should
deteriorate into farcical muddle of the *Handy Andy* variety. It
was, after all, a mere eight years earlier that Maria Edgeworth

had insisted that 'we are in too perilous a case to laugh, humour would be out of season, worse than bad taste.' By her lights, Lover's *Handy Andy* must be one of the notable examples of novelistic bad taste. Here again, of course, we encounter the shaping influence of those English readers with a very limited tolerance of Irish novels which forced the grim realities of the country upon them. An English novelist, who made his first essays in the form during his stay in Ireland, was to be made sharply aware of this by a reprimand from a reviewer in the *Athenaeum*. Anthony Trollope, who had come to Ireland as Deputy Postal Surveyor in 1841 and had lived through the horrors of the Famine, published in 1847 a very fine first novel, *The Macdermots of Ballycloran,* in which he displayed considerable sympathy for and genuine understanding of the plight of Irish Catholics and the tortuous dangers of Ribbonism. The reviewer in the *Athenaeum* commented coldly: 'An Irish novel has become to us something like the haunted chest in the corner of Merchant Abudah's apartment, which even when closed we know to contain a shape of Terror and a voice of Woe! Nor will *The Macdermots of Ballycloran* disenchant anyone from a reluctance engendered like our own.'[7]

Trollope who, even at that early stage, was already attentive to the demands of his public, took the hint and his later Irish novels, *The Kellys and the O'Kellys* (1848) and *Castle Richmond* (1860) are entertaining novels of manners rather than profound explorations of Irish tragedy. Charles Lever, for whom Trollope expressed a warm affection, took an opposite direction, moving from gaiety to gravity. He had come to novel-writing by chance, when he found that *The Confessions of Harry Lorrequer* went down well in serial form in the *Dublin University Magazine*. He was to go on to produce many novels which could only be classed as high-spirited entertainments but some of his more mature work, in novels such as *The Knight of Gwynne* (1845), *The Martins of Cro'Martin* (1856) and his last novel of all, *Lord Kilgobbin* (1872), were of a much more serious nature. He is a writer who has been seriously underestimated and is long overdue for revaluation. The fact that he remained a Tory in politics did not blind him to the miseries of the Irish poor and he was a perceptive recorder of the peculiar stresses and strains of the Ascendancy Big House, a capacity he shares with his contemporary, Sheridan Le Fanu and his successors, Somerville and Ross. It might have seemed that the wealthy residences of the Anglo-Irish gentry provided islands of calm in the turbulence of the period and Yeats was later to wax nostalgic about them, celebrating 'Great windows open to the south' and deploring the mindless destruction of the cultural accumulation of the years. Curiously, though, the novels which came out of this setting are far from serene. At their best, in works such as Lever's *The Martins of Cro'Martin* or George Moore's *A Drama in Muslin* or Somerville and Ross's *The Real Charlotte,* the writers expose the fundamental unease of Ireland's ruling class and their strange, in-between world, halfway between two cultures. Elizabeth Bowen, herself a later and richly talented representative of the type, was to claim that Bartram Haugh, the mysterious and menacing house at the heart of Le Fanu's best-known novel, *Uncle Silas* (1864), was really an Irish gentry house transferred to an English setting and W. J. McCormack's recent valuable study of Le Fanu and his period makes clear the powerful influence exerted on Le Fanu's later development by his troubled childhood in a country house beset by fears of hostile forces outside.[8] Le Fanu's is one of the stranger and more private imaginations at work in the third quarter of the century. One of the great ghost story writers and author of James Joyce's favourite novel, *The House by the Churchyard,* the 'Invisible Prince', as he was known to his Dublin neighbours, reflects in his personal dark privacy the peculiar tensions of his tribe.

When W. B. Yeats published his *Irish Representative Tales* in 1891, he differentiated between what he called 'two different accents, the accent of the gentry and the less polished accent of the peasantry and those close to them.' This is a convenient oversimplification and, while one sees what Yeats means, his categorisation should not blind us to the fact that all the nineteenth century writers, whether from Big House or cabin, from the emergent Catholic middle-class or the declining Protestant Ascendancy, were subject to similar creative pressures. The 'gentry' writers might view Ireland from a somewhat different angle from that adopted by the writers

with 'the less polished accents of the peasantry' but both kinds
of writer lived in the same troubled island and both had to
work hard in their courting of a foreign audience. Both also
had to accept inevitable criticism of their rendering of Irish
life and character. Some were accused of condescending to
the Irish people, others of sentimentalising them. Some were
silenced by Irish reality, others took refuge from it in a humour
which deteriorated into escapist farce. William Carleton, most
considerable of the native novelists, surveyed the scene and,
in his autobiography, gloomily prophesied: 'Banim and
Griffin are gone, and I will soon follow them – *ultimus
Romanorum,* and after that will come a lull, an obscurity of
perhaps half a century. . ."' If we understand that Carleton
had in mind writers such as Banim, Griffin and himself,
writers who sprang from the people and knew their intimate
miseries, we must grant that his prophecy was to prove largely
true. Among the native writers of the post-Famine period one
searches in vain for a worthy successor to the William Carleton
who had dubbed himself both the 'great peasant' and the Irish
Scott. Only Charles Kickham, perhaps, comes easily to mind,
though he is a lesser talent than Carleton. His much-loved
Knocknagow (1879) was to find its way into the affections of
the Irish people in spite of its melodrama and sentimentality
because, in the midst of all that, it also offered a touchingly
convincing portrayal of Irish country people and places, of
the rural pursuits of the Irish poor and the dire predicament
of a doomed community. Its essential and enduring qualities
can be discerned if the novel is contrasted with a novel of the
same period in which the harsh realities of the time are
conveyed through the eyes of a talented woman writer from
an Ascendancy background, Emily Lawless, daughter of Lord
Cloncurry. Her vigorous novel, *Hurrish* (1886), has in it much
in the way of scenic description and vivid action which holds
the attention of the modern reader but the book is spoilt again
and again by tedious and tasteless editorialising which
oversimplifies characters into stereotypes and smacks of an
irritating assumption of superiority on the part of the writer
herself. Her creative vision is blurred again and again by the
political shorthand of her class, while Kickham, though he
falls into regrettable failures of sensibility and knows little

about handling a plot, never distances himself from his fictional people in a similarly damaging manner and so, in spite of his excessive length and lapses into melodrama and sentimentality, retains our sympathies and affection to the end.

It has sometimes been suggested that the Irish fiction of the nineteenth century is something of a hybrid, bearing little relation to Irish writing in the present century. This view may derive from the radical political changes which have taken place in the interval. An Ireland which has turbulently achieved some measure of political independence and has begun to strive to take its proper place in the world and articulate its views and attitudes independently, tends to look back on the harrowing miseries and struggles of the previous century and see them as 'old forgotten far-off things and battles long ago'. The novels and stories themselves, however, may here and there suggest that no such simple division exists between the two centuries. The Irish writers' continuing fondness for the short story form and the tendency of many modern Irish writers to disrupt the normal patterns of the traditional novel in various spirited ways must, one feels, derive in some fashion from the creative struggles of their nineteenth century predecessors who so often struggled to impose inappropriately decorous forms on recalcitrant materials. Modern Irish writers have carried on a tradition of verbal comedy initiated by Carleton's polysyllabic polymaths and Griffin's hedge-school hilarities. The verbal high-jinks of *Finnegans Wake* and *At Swim-Two-Birds* are not without ancestry in the earlier period. On the level of dark realism, one discerns an evident kinship between John Banim's tormented hero, John Nowlan, and the anguished protagonist of John McGahern's novel, *The Dark*. Consider also the surprising vitality in the modern period of the 'Big House' genre, a form of the novel which might have been thought to have passed away with the decline of the class which inspired it. Yet, writers as varied as Jennifer Johnston, Aidan Higgins, John Banville and Caroline Blackwood have revived this kind of fiction in the recent past with quite remarkable success. The nineteenth century, it would seem, can still speak to us meaningfully through its novels and short stories and it is to be hoped that the many lively and enterprising publishing houses which have sprung up in Ireland in recent years will contribute to a revival of interest in the fiction of the last century by reprinting some of the more important works of the period, many of which have long been unobtainable.

2. George Moore and his Irish Novels

Richard Allen Cave

When W. B. Yeats compiled his anthology, *Representative Irish Tales* (1891), he selected Rosa Mulholland as the only living exponent of the art of fiction. Wilde was omitted; so too was George Moore, despite his having recently published a profound and wide-ranging novel of Irish life, *A Drama in Muslin* (1886). Possible reasons for the omission are legion. Moore's work did not fit comfortably into Yeats's thesis that there are two distinct accents in Irish literature: 'the accent of the gentry and the less polished accent of the peasantry. . . a division roughly into the voice of those who lived lightly and gayly, and those who took man and his fortunes with much seriousness and even at times mournfully.'[1] Then again Moore's claim to be working under the influence of the French novelist Zola laid him open to suspicion (Zola's English publisher, Vizetelly, had been gaoled for issuing work deemed scandalous and improper); Susan Mitchell tells us that Yeats had forbidden his sister to read Moore's previous novel, *A Mummer's Wife* (1885), though the ban served only to excite her curiosity: 'With femine perversity. . . I gulped guilty pages of it as I went to bed of nights.'[2] To her great surprise she found the experience far from titillating; it was unredeemably *moral*. Throughout his career Moore's best novels – *Esther Waters,* his tale of an unmarried servant-girl and her illegitimate child, and his historical romances based on the life of Christ (*The Brook Kerith*) and of Héloïse and Abélard – question conventional unthinking moral attitudes and assert richer, because more discriminating, values. 'Moral' is perhaps a dangerous word to apply to a novelist: it risks suggesting his work is prone to dullness, the drily sententious, an over-reliance on a commentary heavy with abstractions and generalisations, a plot-line carefully shaped to illustrate a given thesis and so lacking in narrative excitement. 'Moral' and 'discriminating' might seem peculiarly unapt epithets to apply to Moore who in his public life and especially in Dublin delighted in playing the fool to discomfort the pompous and the serious-minded. The popular myths about Moore the man do not match well with the personality of his writing self; yet both selves share one common feature: a tremendous joy in life that fuelled a detestation of stuffy, out-moded, deadly patterns of behaviour. In his novels Moore did not start with a clearly formulated idea of what he wished the fiction to demonstrate or prove; writing for him rather was a process of discovery about a character, and he invites his reader to engage imaginatively with that character to the same challenging degree so that as the circumstances of the plot bring the hero or heroine to a full awareness of his or her moral identity so the reader's powers of discrimination are more sensitively tuned. Moore's best novels are adventures in the mind and sensibility for character, author and reader alike. *A Drama in Muslin,* Moore's first Irish novel, would not fit Yeats's thesis of what constitutes the representative in Irish fiction because it deliberately searches for a moral code beyond those two 'accents' of gentry and peasant, because such styles of fiction carry predictable, inherited attitudes (especially about social and class issues) and evoke in the reader relaxed expectations that are quickly satisfied. Moore wanted a relationship with his reader that was frankly exploratory and creative. *A Drama in Muslin* sets out to question by what right in fact the gentry live 'lightly and gayly' while the lot of the peasant is perennially 'mournful'.

The novel is set in near-contemporaneous times and is directed at examining what Moore recognised would in retrospect be seen as a significant point of change in Ireland's social history, when the activities of the Land League began seriously to challenge the power of the landlords. As the League's work in Mayo drastically affected Moore's rents from his own estate in the country compelling him to abandon a carefree Bohemian existence in Paris and indeed take to novel-writing to supplement his income, one might have expected the attitude and approach of *A Drama in Muslin* to be partisan and the tone somewhat shrill. But this is not the case. Moore at no time sought police protection or went about armed when he returned to Moore Hall in the winter of 1880-

81; amongst the neighbouring gentry he was considered in fact a dangerous radical. The novel explains why, for it is meticulously objective in its viewpoint. Moore takes the need for a moral stance seriously and defines it with care.

What impresses on a first reading of *A Drama in Muslin* is the sheer range of reference and Moore's capacity to see a tragic pattern behind the wealth of detail and incident. His focus is predominantly on a cluster of young girls who are coming out in society, attending their first Dublin season and being presented at the Viceregal court. The aim in all their minds is to find a husband with a position that guarantees their future security and to do so quickly before the bloom of youth fades. Trained to be demure in their convent school, they now learn how to sustain and project that quality but artfully as a means of making themselves agreeable to men; mothers and chaperones set to and instruct them how to be at once alluring and virginal, to cultivate 'an air of falseness as indescribable as it was bewitching.'[3] The ideal is set by Mrs Barton, the heroine's mother, whose 'figure was singularly in keeping with her moral character; both were elegant, refined, supple.'[4] How cleverly Moore shifts his ground with that last epithet exposing the ideal as suddenly shoddy! The pressures on the girls to find security are acute, so a spirit of great competitiveness is quickly generated amongst them; envy and rancour are soon allowed full play and the relations between the girls become covertly spiteful. The demure public appearance disguises in most of them a hard, calculating temperament that is not above malice or scandal–mongering. As the season wears on and the chances of many fade, they give way to a bitter peevishness that finds relief only in retailing gossip about the failures of others. The pattern of the season sets the pattern of their lives. 'Are such women, ladies?' Alice Barton questions, astonished at even her sister's decline into abusing a rival's character. Moore's handling of dialogue and the rapid delineation of character through idiosyncrasies of speech is a recurrent strength in his writing and he charts that decline in the girls through their talk with a sharply accurate ear from the naïve to the cleverly cajoling affected in the company of men to the downright coarse in private: 'I assure you I know lots of girls – and very nice girls too – who have been going out these six or seven seasons, and who have not been able to pull it off.'[5]

To fit out the girls and their chaperones in the finery required for attendance at a state levée or ball incurs exorbitant costs in clothing, the taking of rooms in the Shelbourne Hotel for the season or the renting of a well-situated house. And it is here that Moore's larger social theme is sounded. Like Zola, Moore is adept at evoking through a highly charged, impressionistic prose a sense of outrage at massive and conspicuous waste. The elegance has its price in financial as well as psychological and moral terms. To preserve this glittering façade that defines one's rank and social position requires money, and money in this context means rents. It is to Moore's credit that he did not at this point resort to too rigid and simplistic a standpoint; his imaginative engagement with his subject is subtle in its range of sympathies. Vain, empty-headed, unprincipled, even vicious though the girls are seen to be, they nonetheless excite Moore's pity as the victims of circumstance. They have inherited a way of life that has been the unchallenged *status quo* for generations; irresponsible they certainly are, but not from conscious moral choice; they have never been taught to question or even to look beyond the gratification of the present moment because the future was always believed to be secure. That is what preserving a woman's innocence amounted to. But the Land League has begun to undermine the system of land-tenure and rents on which the whole superstructure of rank is founded and, if in the present season the women's man-hunting has become more desperate, it is because they have come to realise the possibility of a future that is unpredictable, indeed terrifying in its uncertainties. Few have the imagination or stamina necessary to create an alternative life-style; as Moore comments: 'What could they do with their empty brains? What could they do with their feeble hands?'[6] Moore accepts that change is necessary, but he recognises that it too has its price in terms of human suffering.

The spiritual poverty of the gentry is matched in Moore's view by the physical degradation of the peasants whom the renting exploits. A chilling feature to the modern reader of the novel is Moore's depiction of the way the gentry have scarcely noticed the presence of the peasants in the landscape of their demesnes, so assured have they been of the perpetuation of the *status quo*; but the agrarian crisis has thrust the poor to the forefront of their consciousness; conspicuous everywhere, the peasants stand out starkly now against the landscape as a reality and a potent threat. Occasionally the incongruities and contrasts of the lives of rich and poor excite Moore to an impassioned rhetoric about social inequalities, but generally he impresses the idea more powerfully on the reader's imagination by simply juxtaposing facts and insights about the two ways of life, their relative degrees of misery, envy and fear, which leaves the reader creatively to respond and find his own measure of enlightenment or shock. Mrs Barton's dismissal of a suitor for one of her daughters because his income in her view is insufficient to maintain Olive in an 'agreeable' condition cross-cuts into a confrontation between Mr Barton and his tenant-farmers about the value of the rents that are to pay for Olive's first Dublin season and her hunt for a title; when a county ball is held, the dancers suddenly are aware of the gaunt faces of the poor staring in at them through the misted windows; as their carriages advance in the rain to the Castle, the headlights catch briefly in vivid detail abject, silent observers of their progress – the inhabitants of Dublin's tenements. Terrified that this might be an image of their own future, the gentry become vindictive and petty; lacking imaginative engagement with the poor they remain politically ineffective: that what has always been is right is clearly no adequate defense of their position; incapable of uniting on viable moral grounds against the League, they are routed and destined to suffer change. Moore makes no detailed case for the Land League; his novel offers a comprehensive range of social facts and presents the League as the agent of change.

It is fitting to discuss *A Drama in Muslin* in a course of lectures of modern Irish fiction partly because it deals with political activity that contributed greatly to the shaping of modern Ireland, but also because in the presentation of one character – Alice Barton – Moore fashioned a technique for rendering an adventure in consciousness that was to affect both his own future development as a novelist and in some

measure the course of twentieth-century Irish fiction. Alice is
the first of Moore's characters to undergo a revolution in
sensibility; the pressures which mould her sister and her
contemporaries into tragic victims strengthen her resilience
and excite in her the courage to renounce a way of life that is
troubling to her conscience and her keen sense of integrity;
she learns how to accept change as part of the process that is
history. Conscious that she is plain in comparison with her
sister Olive, Alice has a modesty that is genuine, not a veneer;
she has considerable intelligence and a creative imagination
that refuse to allow her to accept her parents' attitudes as a
pointless expression of duty; she judges all experience freshly
and on its own terms. To her mother's chagrin, she tries to
show that the peasants have a case that is worth putting;
finding the Viceregal season trivial and husband-hunting an
insult to her integrity, she begins to create a private moral
identity for herself within, till circumstances help her to find
an outlet for that new self in writing as a career. Moore does
not sentimentalise his heroine: she is not a successful writer,
no over-night success, but her competence allows her to be
independent of a world that has grown to sicken her morally.
It is through his depiction of Alice's awakening conscience
that Moore guides the reader towards a sensitive and clearsighted appraisal of the social tragedy at the heart of his novel.
Ultimately Alice chooses exile to safeguard her independence
as a writer. For her no more than for Joyce's Stephen Dedalus
in *A Portrait of the Artist* is exile merely a carefree escape from
an oppressive past. Like Stephen, in her darker moods she
wishes she could flee the nightmare that is history, but she
chooses to work to shape her own destiny. She too acquires
the courage to be true to herself and the stamina to work to
perfect her independent vision in her art; viewing the poverty
about her and discovering its cause, she has already learned
more than Stephen 'what the heart is and what it feels'. The
strength of Moore's novel is that it shows us how is forged
in the smithy of Alice's soul the (till now) uncreated conscience
of her race.[7] Moore's first major novel finds its greatness in
being a novel *about* Ireland, *for* Ireland.

That it is 'wrong to withhold our sympathy from any side
of life'[8] is an innate belief in Alice, and *A Drama in Muslin* is

much taken up with her struggles to preserve its truth against pressures to conform to more prejudiced values. For Father Oliver Gogarty in Moore's later Irish novel *The Lake* (1905, revised 1921) the idea of a need to keep open a flow of generous sympathy in judging all experience in life is not instinctive, it grows in him to the strength of a conviction as a consequence of a series of awakenings that cause him to question the whole basis of his vocation as a country parson. At the climax of the novel, anxious to spare his congregation from any scandal, Father Gogarty abandons his clerical garb beside the lake that is the boundary of his parish, swims across during the night and departs to seek a new life in America leaving the Mayo villagers to suppose him drowned. Once again exile is grasped as the only possible conclusion to the spiritual renaissance Gogarty undergoes. Gogarty like Alice has no resting place in Ireland till the country experiences change, finding a more relaxed and generous social tone. If Moore's overall theme again anticipates Joyce, the particular technique he evolves to dramatise that theme in the mind-life of his priest anticipates much that is characteristic of Beckett's work. *The Lake* is essentially about the workings of conscience to bring a broken, restless mind to health. Gogarty has denounced vigorously from his altar a young woman, Nora Glynn, whom gossip has reported is carrying an illegitimate child; the woman has disappeared and is believed drowned. Some months later a London priest writes confirming Nora's safety; Gogarty begs her address; he apologises for his past conduct and a correspondence ensues, brief on her part, lengthy on his, in which he examines his past and recognises that his every action till now has been governed by a suppression of his instinctive self, a deliberate withholding of sympathy. Seeking forgiveness of her, he finds a greater need to forgive himself if he is to recover any vestige of integrity. Conscience in Gogarty is presented by Moore as an irresistible urge coming from deep in the subliminal reaches of the priest's mind that compels him relentlessly to tell over and over again to his consciousness the story of his public attack on Nora and its consequences. The mind is insistent that he recognise his betrayal of his own best self. Only by determined efforts of concentration can he temporarily still that voice; the instant he relaxes his willed control over the drift of his thoughts, it reasserts its power. When first we encounter Gogarty he is strolling in the woods that border the lake; his attention to details in the landscape and the natural life about him is almost obsessive; he pursues at length memories that the place evokes of his childhood and adolescence; and fantasises longingly about the destination of a yacht he catches sight of. Seeing the schoolhouse where Nora formerly taught, he finally admits that 'all the morning he had been trying to keep Nora Glynn out of his mind.'[9] But now the tale begins to be told again inexorably. As the days pass he dreads it beginning afresh and fears waking to find it already in possession of his consciousness: 'It was his elbow companion in the evening as he sat smoking his pipe, and every morning as he stood at the end of a sandy spit seeing nothing, hearing nothing but her.'[10] There seems no point to the endless repetitions and he muses whether in time he could become inured to the process and go through it without pain. (The parallel with Beckett's *Eh Joe* is particularly exact.)

The technique is a good one, presenting the reader with necessary exposition about Gogarty's past at a point where his life is verging on change. Re-telling Nora's story is not, however, done in a way that invites monotony; with each telling the emphasis falls differently as if the mind like an artist is trying to find the most pleasing and satisfying account. When the knowledge comes that Nora is alive Gogarty has to explain himself both to Father O'Grady, the London priest, and to Nora by way of apology; that her view of their shared past differs from his requires Gogarty to think the story through again from a perspective more sympathetic to Nora. The story must be told aright before his conscience will allow him freedom; the pattern is one of purgatory and redemption with the mind acting as its own confessor and judge. The exactness and variety of subtly differing prose styles Moore brings to the depiction of Gogarty's spiritual progress is remarkable; so scrupulous does his own judging mind become in viewing the flow of his thoughts and associations that the reader is compelled to read with as fine an eye for detail; Moore never tells us how to relate to Gogarty in the stages of his mental torment and release, rather through his style he invites us to engage imaginatively with that mind in its sickness and quest for recovery.

But it would be wrong to imply that Moore achieves such an engagement with his character's consciousness exclusively through the device of telling over Nora's story. Certainly that provides the novel with its overall structure; but Moore obviously saw the need for variety of pace to allow his reader time to gauge the changing quality of Gogarty's sensibility. When Moore returned to Ireland in 1901 after many years in England and on the continent living in sophisticated literary and artistic circles that had become increasingly claustrophobic, he was particularly struck, as he recounts in his autobiography, *Hail and Farewell,* by the freshness and clarity of the landscape and the quality of the light. The Ireland he had been fond of dismissing as a place of weed and ruin suddenly reinvigorated his spirit. He took to walking, rejoicing in the beauties of natural things and this private epiphany found expression in a much purer, simpler style than that he had affected in the nineties. Direct, unadorned, it nonetheless achieves a remarkable degree of poetic resonance. This is the style he strengthened and perfected through the composition of the tales that make up *The Untilled Field;* in *The Lake* he employs it with the skill of a virtuoso.[11] *The Lake*, Moore was fond of claiming in later years, was his 'landscape book'. Made restless by the worries nagging in his head, Father Gogarty escapes to the lakes and woods that skirt his parish; at first a necessary distraction, the landscape comes to captivate his interest more deeply as he appreciates that it can actually enhance his developing self-awareness. If on one level *The Lake* is about conscience; it is also about perception – how one's mode of perception is indicative of the quality of one's sensibility. Gogarty's adventure in the mind takes him through states of guilt, remorse, acceptance, confession, absolution, rebirth; but these states are not *explained* by Moore, rather they are evoked through the manner in which at any given time Gogarty chooses to tell Nora's story to himself and how he responds to the natural world about him as he does so. When he is plunged into remorse and a morbid self-pity, the landscape becomes a sinister, melodramatic place that conjures forth in his mind tortuous images of death; exploring these images, he recognises that they are 'far-fetched and unhealthy',[12] which causes him to ponder why his mind has succumbed to such affectation. If guilt and remorse are no more than mannerisms, then he must journey on and find his truth to himself elsewhere. As his mind frees itself of the burden of guilt so his perceptions are cleansed and restored to a primal innocence of vision. By the time that Gogarty has freed himself of inveterate habits of thinking and feeling and learned to trust his instinctive self, Nora's story has become 'a song in the head' celebrating his release from the hide-bound, dogmatic religion he formerly practised and his discovery of a more rewarding faith based on a reverence for whatever is life-enhancing. That new-found joy seeks expression in a loving appraisal of the Irish countryside:

> He walked along the foreshore feeling like an instrument that had been tuned. His perception seemed to have been indefinitely increased, and it seemed to him as if he were in communion with the stones in the earth and the clouds in heaven; it seemed to him as if the past and the future had become one.
>
> The moment was one of extraordinary sweetness. . . . And he watched the earth and sky enfolded in one tender harmony of rose and blue – blue fading to gray, and the lake afloat amid vague shores, receding like a dream through sleep.[13]

The Lake is the first novel of consciousness in English; it is a book about the landscape of the mind that celebrates the landscape of the Irish countryside for its power to condition the Irish soul. Gogarty enters his adult life a victim of cerebral moral values; as he opens himself up increasingly to the truth of what his perceptions reveal so he finds a complete integrity in letting the forces of his subliminal self more creatively shape his personality. Gogarty finally acknowledges: '"There is a lake in every man's heart. . . and he listens to its monotonous whisper year by year, more and more attentive till at last he ungirds".'[14] Through metaphor, perception has become vision and a philosophy of life. The Lake is Moore's masterpiece and his most profoundly Irish novel; it set a pattern for the landscape of Irish fiction in the present century.

3. The Short Story: 1900–1945

Colbert Kearney

My topic is the work of those Irish short story writers who were published before the end of the Second World War. Given the space at my disposal, I have decided to concentrate on authors rather than on individual stories. Even then I have had to be selective and I am uncomfortably conscious of the fact that I have omitted some writers whose absence could hardly be justified in a more leisurely account of the Irish short story.

Although we all use the term 'short story' quite casually, nobody has yet come up with a definition which is both precise and practical. What we call a short story, though it is obviously a descendant of the folktale, began to assume its characteristic form in the nineteenth century. There were many reasons for this, not the least important of which was the growing popularity of magazines and periodicals which contained an assortment of short contributions – poems, memoirs, descriptive articles, essays, reviews, letters and tales. Another influence was the surge of democratic feeling: members of the educated minority began to show a new concern for the lower orders and a new interest in their culture, hitherto dismissed as contemptible.

Take the case of Ivan Turgenev whose book *Sketches from a Hunter's Album* is among the greatest collections of short stories. Turgenev was an aristocrat who published these sketches in periodicals in the mid-nineteenth century. They introduced the reader to the characters and landscapes of Russian serfdom. The pose as a hunter helps to explain the familiarity of the narrator with the world of the serfs. In Czarist Russia the serfs were treated as useful adjuncts of the ruling class and they occupied a similar place in literature; to suggest otherwise was to risk the displeasure of the authorities and Turgenev was suspected of political subversion. He was one of several great Russian writers who described the life of the poor without the traditional condescension and in doing so gave to literature a sense of the short story as a brief narrative which concentrated on the lives of the lower orders who had until then been more or less excluded from serious literature.

The history of short fiction in Ireland parallels that of mainland Europe. The folktale has always been an important ingredient. So too has been the desire to explore and explain the charm and squalor of low life in town and countryside. Early in the nineteenth century Thomas Crofton Croker had a huge success with an anthology of folklore which he called *Fairy Legends and Traditions of the South of Ireland*. His even more interesting contemporary was William Carleton whose career epitomises many of the conflicts which unbalanced Irish cultural life in the nineteenth century. The heir to an oral Gaelic tradition, he became a considerable writer in English. At one time destined for the Catholic priesthood, some of his best work was intended as an exposure of the evil influence of the Catholic clergy in Ireland. He aspired to write novels in the English manner but his reputation rests on shorter works which are closer to storytelling in the Irish mode. In *Traits and Stories of the Irish Peasantry*, Carleton the sophisticated narrator, invites the reader into the obscurity of the Irish cabin consciousness, a consciousness which Carleton understood only too well for his own comfort. Happily, his delight in the crazier colours of character and language subverted his didactic zeal and he created a world of exuberant and squalid innocence which retains its power to charm and chill the modern reader.

Another kind of innocence is associated with Edith Somerville and Violet Martin, two Anglo-Irish ladies who became famous as Somerville and Ross. In 1898 they began to publish a series of tales entitled *Some Adventures of an Irish R.M.* which presented a deliciously comic view of the world they knew so well – the 'county' world of the decrepit gentry, the intractable peasantry and the horse-dealers who dominate the middle ground. To what was then a traditional form – Ireland seen through the bemused eyes of a surprisingly innocent Englishman – Somerville and Ross brought a sharpness of insight, an uncanny ear for speech, an irresistible sense of fun and a general lightness of touch which remains unique in Irish writing.

I prefer to see the development of the Irish short story in the context of nineteenth-century literary history but it would be possible to argue that the modern Irish short story sprang fully formed from the head of George Moore. Having no interest in the family estate in Mayo, Moore had made his way to Paris. Having failed to make it as a painter, he became a very successful novelist with a reputation for dealing with such dangerous themes as sex and class. In 1901, at the height of his fame, Moore accepted Yeats's invitation to lend his support to the Irish literary revival. His most helpful contribution was a collection of short stories, published in 1903 and entitled *The Untilled Field*. Moore was happy to acknowledge his debt to his friend Turgenev and many of the stories deal with the peasants of rural Ireland in a manner which recalls Turgenev.

The title points to the rural Irish parish, characterised by physical and emotional under-development, a field which remains untilled by edict of the repressive priest. Moore's stories are typical of the modern short story in many ways. They focus on characters who would not have been treated seriously in contemporary fiction. They stress idiosyncrasies of behaviour and speech and, because they deal with a society which is repressed – whether by actual tyranny or by isolation – they contain an element of social protest. For Moore, the priests who condemned the peasants to a life of deprivation were more reprehensible then the most benighted landowners in Turgenev's Russia.

Many of the stories operate in an area defined by marriage, Maynooth and America. One alternative to a loveless marriage arranged by the priest is emigration to America; another is the cultivation of a religious vocation. In one of the stories, 'Home Sickness', an Irishman leaves the unhealthy squalor of New York to find his health at home in Ireland; there he falls in love with a beautiful woman but, rather than accept the puritanical regime imposed by the local priest, he returns to New York. The dullest of lives in the Bowery is more tolerable, he implies, than life in the most beautiful part of Ireland.

Some of the material recalls Carleton but there is no confusing the styles. Moore is always confident and controlled. From his limp sentences to his overall construction he writes with the weight of the European tradition behind him and nowhere is this more obvious than when he deals with the folklore and speech of the Irish tradition as, for example, in 'The Wedding Gown' or in what is probably the finest story of the collection, 'The Window'. This tells of an old woman who is obsessed with the idea of presenting a stained-glass window to a new church. When she lapses into insanity she becomes the focus of a local cult and this excess of religious passion is contrasted with the routine observances of the priest.

While Moore was establishing the rural short story, two Dubliners, both of whom will be the subjects of later lectures, were doing the same for the urban story. In 1905 James Stephens published his first story. A year earlier James Joyce had begun to write those stories which would eventually be published as *Dubliners*.

Joyce saw the city of Dublin as an untilled field or, in terms closer to his own, as a back-garden reeking of weeds and ashpits. He also referred to it as a victim of paralysis, a word which fascinated the narrator of the opening story: 'It filled me with fear, and yet I longed to be near to it and to look upon its deadly work.' The city of these stories is a lower middle-class world of graceless torpor in which human enterprise is stifled by a moral climate of fear and entrapment. Mr Doran is checkmated into marriage by his mother-in-law-to-be, a butcher's daughter who deals with moral problems as a cleaver deals with meat. Mr Farington, seething with dissatisfaction after a day of defeats, savages his own son, deaf to his appeals: '"O pa!" he cried. "Don't beat me, pa! And I'll. . . I'll say a *Hail Mary* for you. . . I'll say a *Hail Mary* for you, pa, if you don't beat me. . .I'll say a Hail Mary. . ."'[1] Not surprisingly, some early readers found Joyce's vision depressingly grim. Some denounced his realism as obscene while others were unhappy with what they took to be structural weaknesses. Today we would dismiss any suggestion of technical inadequacy and would claim that the tone is not one of unrelieved gloom. Yet we should realise that we too would have been unsettled to encounter stories by an unknown writer who refused to grant the reader such traditional assurances as a clear narrative voice and an eventful plot complete with beginning, middle and conclusive ending. It is only in our own time that critics have produced a criticism which can adequately account for Joyce's achievement.

Joyce makes frequent use of what is often called 'focalised' narrative. Basically, this means that Joyce avoids adopting a traditional narrator's voice and prefers to allow the narrative to take its colouring from the character involved. When Joyce begins the final story as follows – 'Lily, the caretaker's daughter, was literally run off her feet,'[2] he is not failing to avoid jargon and cliché, he is removing the traditional narrator from between the reader and the action and giving us the action as Lily would experience it. It is partly by means of this technique that Joyce generates the tone of generous satire which is his hallmark and which characterises such comic masterpieces as 'Clay'.

Towards the end of this story, the maiden aunt Maria obliges the Hallowe'en party with her rendering of 'I Dreamt that I Dwelt', but apparently she gets it wrong. The narrator does not say how or why. The reader must discover that she has failed to sing of the suitors who sought her hand and must then decide whether she avoided this verse intentionally or because she was a little tipsy or because of some subconscious aversion. The story concludes with the reaction of her brother Joe: 'No one tried to show her her mistake; and when she had ended her song Joe was very much moved. He said that there was no time like the long ago and no music for him like poor old Balfe, whatever other people might say; and his eyes filled up so much with tears that he could not find what he was looking for and in the end he had to ask his wife to tell him where the corkscrew was.'[3] In its clearsighted generosity and its humane comedy, this seems to me as close to perfection as literature ever gets.

It could be argued that Joyce's work did not exercise a major influence on the Irish short story until after the Second World War, that in the years between the wars the more effective and controversial presence was that of Daniel Corkery.

In 1907 Corkery noted that he knew nothing of the Irish peasant because 'our Irish peasants have not got into print.'[4] It was not the case that Corkery, a man of wide reading, was unaware of the efforts of earlier writers such as George Moore, but Corkery believed that only those who shared the three main concerns of Irish life – Nationalism, Religion and Land – could express the life of Ireland in literature and this excluded such writers as Somerville and Ross, Moore, Yeats and others of the Anglo-Irish ascendancy who tended to be unionist, Protestant and landowning. Though his ideological position and his consequent criticism are often suspect, some of Corkery's stories are very fine and his general contribution to the Irish short story was considerable.

It is often forgotten that about half of Corkery's first collection, *A Munster Twilight* (1916), consists of stories set in the slums of Cork city which, in their grim humour, grotesque images and characters, suggest the influence of Gogol. Unfortunately, Corkery did not persist with this material. Instead, he concentrated on stories of rural life and so well did he suggest the countryside of the Cork/Kerry border that some readers thought his name was a pseudonym based on the words Cork and Kerry. Corkery introduces his reader to the characters and culture of rural Ireland much as Turgenev introduced his readers to rural Russia. His perception of rural life was influenced by another of his favourite Russians, Gorky. It was the elemental quality of peasant life which fascinated the quiet, city-bred teacher and which gave some of his stories a primitive energy.

The land itself is the principal agency of his writings. The lives of his characters are a dour struggle against the resisting earth, a perpetual toil in thin fields littered with stones – stones piled into walls, stones associated with traditional pieties, stones still in the positions they had assumed before the arrival of human life. Fittingly, perhaps his best story is called 'The Stones'. It comes from his 1929 collection, *The Stormy Hills* – a tale of natural magic which suggests with uncanny power the relationship between the landscape and the mind of man.

Corkery was a major influence on many younger writers who admired his ability to write of Irish life with a balanced sympathy which was often at odds with the extreme position he took in his critical writings. Perhaps his most significant contribution was his invention of a narrative voice which was neither that of master nor servant and which would seem the natural voice of the new Free State.

Michael O'Donovan, better known as Frank O'Connor, was born to extremely poor parents in Cork in 1903. Inspired by Corkery, who was his teacher inside and outside the classroom, O'Connor became a student of culture, both the high culture of Europe and the traditional Irish culture which the Gaelic League was trying to resuscitate. Directed by Corkery, O'Connor explored that substratum of Irish life which was still shaped by the Gaelic tradition but which had yet to find expression in modern Irish literature. The Gaelic literary tradition had survived principally in oral form and the most immediately striking characteristic of O'Connor's genius is his ability to transcribe an oral style, to get tones of voice onto the printed page. Whether it be with the inflexions of a precocious young boy persecuted by the female sex or those of an old farmer whose mind has been weathered by age, O'Connor's prose speaks to us with unerring intimacy.

It was with Corkery's encouragement that O'Connor became involved in the War of Independence and in the Civil War but it was in defiance of his master that O'Connor expressed his dissatisfaction with the new Ireland and began to write stories which focused on the less glorious aspects of the military struggle and the less admirable fruits of political independence. One of his earliest stories, 'Guests of the Nation', is considered a classic account of men at war. Some of his best stories dramatise the conflict between the older Ireland and the new. A masterpiece in this vein is 'The Majesty of the Law'. Another is 'The Long Road to Ummera', a moving account of an old woman's determination not to be buried in the city where her son has prospered in business but in the country district where she was born. 'Musha, take me back to Ummera, Pat,' she whined. 'Take me back to my own. I'd never rest among strangers. I'd be rising and drifting.'[5] Many of O'Connor's later stories deal with people who are left lonely or embittered by repressive social codes and with children as the victims of adult wars. Our sense of childhood in Ireland owes more than a little to O'Connor whose fictionalised accounts of his own early days on the Northside in Cork are among the best and best-loved in Irish writing.

In terms of literary relations O'Connor's twin brother is Sean O'Faolain. Both grew up in Cork, both came under the influence of Corkery, both became disenchanted with the state they had helped bring into existence, both have written prolifically and in a variety of forms, both have excelled in the short story. They are not, however, identical twins. Though drawn to the same themes as O'Connor – memories of childhood, growing up in political turmoil, the isolation of priests and other loners, the changing nature of Irish society – O'Faolain's approach is more intellectual. If O'Connor's work recalls the oral tale, O'Faolain's tends towards philosophical analysis. Stories like 'Midsummer Night Madness' and 'The Silence of the Valley' invite the reader to see them as allegories of Irish society. In a symbolic setting each character speaks for a class or representative point of view. O'Faolain tends to be witty rather than humorous. 'The Man Who Invented Sin' is a droll setting of the Eden theme in an Irish Gaeltacht: a quartet of innocent nuns and brothers are discovered singing on a lake and are expelled from their Munster paradise by a priest whose 'elongated shadow waved behind him like a tail'. Many of his best stories – 'Lovers of the Lake' comes to mind immediately – explore the conflict between the promptings of the flesh and the restraints of religious belief, reminding the reader that O'Faolain belongs to that rare species in Irish writing, the intellectual Catholic. For this and for many other reasons O'Faolain comes across as distinctly European. His later characters tend to be men and women of the world, much travelled, widely read, accustomed to the finer things of life. Their experiences teem with the possessions and passions of the upper middle-classes – cars, clothes, flowers, perfumes, art objects, travel documents, infidelity and leisurely self-scrutiny. In a later version of the religious scruples theme, ironically entitled 'The Faithless Wife', the meagre sexual satisfaction is contrasted with the extravagantly superior consumerism of the Ailesbury Road élite. A diplomat falls for an Irish married woman; 'what had attracted him to her was not only her splendid Boucher figure (whence his sudden nickname for her, La Morphée), or her copper-coloured hair, her lime-green Irish eyes and her seemingly poreless skin, but her calm, total and subdued elegance: the Balenciaga costume, the peacock-skin gloves, the gleaming crocodile handbag, a glimpse of tiny lace-edged lawn handkerchief and her dry, delicate scent. He had a grateful eye and a nose for such things. It was, after all, part of his job. Their second meeting, two weeks later, at his own embassy, has opened the doors. She came alone.'[6] O'Faolain had done much to open out, modernise and internationalise the traditional Irish short story.

The world of Liam O'Flaherty is characteristically primitive. It would seem that his upbringing on the Aran Island has marked his mind and also given him a particularly close sense of the Gaelic storytelling style. Yet he is probably as conscious an artist as O'Faolain. His universe is refined to one of instinctual actions in which man and woman take their places among the other animals. The reader quickly notices how casually O'Flaherty enters the society of animals and how naturally he is attracted to those experiences which human beings share with animals – pain, hunger, fear, courage, strength and the need for ritual. His most famous story is 'Going into Exile' which tells of an American wake for two young people who are leaving some place not unlike the Aran Islands. The narrative is as unsentimental as the characters depicted. Emotions are checked and rechannelled by rituals of resignation. Here are the young man and his father: 'They stood in silence fully five minutes. Each hungered to embrace the other, to cry, to beat the air, to scream with excess of sorrow. But they stood silent and sombre, like nature about them, hugging their woes.'[7] When emotion threatens to burst all bonds it is conducted by means of another ritual – the traditional *caoineadh* – towards a surrender to 'time and patience'. Another fine story which probes a basic instinct – this time it is the religious impulse – is 'The Fairy Goose'. An old woman convinces herself and her neighbours that her ugly gosling is in fact a good fairy but the pleasant delusion is brought to a brutal end when the local priest beats the old woman for her blasphemy and the local lads stone the innocent goose to death. It is with modern eyes that O'Flaherty views his inheritance, those rocky remnants of an older, starker existence. He has little tolerance for those who trespass on his territory in search of footnotes and his comic broadside against such scholarly strangers may be read in his story 'Patsa', unmistakably Gaelic if only for its delight in grotesque detail and vituperation.

How very different from the quieter artistry of Elizabeth Bowen who lived most of her life in England but whose family home was Bowen Court in Cork. Her world is one of nurseries and drawing-rooms and her style offers the satisfaction which a well-kept wine offers the connoisseur. And yet she is quite as elemental in her way as O'Flaherty is in his. Few writers have captured as well as she the isolation which some people – especially children – feel in an unfeeling world.

Can it be that women writers are or were less given to the public clamour? One might say that of Mary Lavin who is largely responsible for adapting the Irish short story to the perspective of Irish women. Her stories have a smooth and superbly detailed texture. She is alert to the least signal – a voice slightly raised, a tablecloth badly ironed. She is a grand master of the chess-games of social intercourse, suggesting the savagery which underlies the conventional exchanges. Read, for example, the dialogue between the two widows in her story 'In a Cafe'. In another story, 'A Tragedy', she shows how domestic discord can overwhelm the heart more cata-strophically than a huge disaster in a neighbouring country. In a rare story with a background of political violence, Matty Conerty acts as a decoy for an IRA man and as he evades the police he feels a sharp pain in his side. 'They got me, he thought, as he fell forward on his face. But the thought did nothing to dispel his elation which seemed only to grow greater. . .'[8] Though the material be unusual the perspective is typical of Mary Lavin. Matty is elated not because he thinks he is dying for Ireland but because he thinks he is escaping the tyranny of his mother. But even in this he is frustrated. He has not been shot; he has merely cut himself on a piece of metal and already his mother is proclaiming his stupidity.

That note of ironic confusion seems a good point on which to end this brief survey of the short story before the War.

4. The Realist Novel: 1900–1945

A. Norman Jeffares

When I was asked to present this piece on *The Realist Novel before the War* my first reaction was to think of Geoge Moore's brilliant picture of Dublin in *Hail and Farewell* (1911, 1912, 1914), that exciting, evocative, entertaining blend of realistic fact and imaginative fiction, and then to think of James Joyce's *Dubliners* (1914), *A Portrait of the Artist as a Young Man* (1916), *Ulysses* (1922) and *Finnegans Wake* (1939) which capture very different aspects of Dublin. But there was a difference in the attitude of these two writers to the countryside, I thought, to the other Ireland. Joyce avoided it, city dweller that he was, but Moore had shown his realistic view of the countryside in the stories of *The Untilled Field* (1903). Then the word 'realist' began to strike home to me, for others were to treat of Moore and Joyce and my brief was to discuss other realistic writers. My mind turned to a wet night in 1915 when Sean O'Faolain saw Lennox Robinson's play *Patriots* on the stage of the Cork Opera House and realised with a shock of recognition that the Ireland he knew could be put on the stage. One of the Cork realists, those early dramatists of the Abbey Theatre, had brought him strange and wonderful news, he thought: that the streets of his native Cork might also be 'full of unsuspected drama'.[1] He was ready, he said, to explore, to respond to, for the first time to see the actuality of life in Ireland. So literature need not be idealistic nor romantic, but could reflect upon and interpret the realities of life.

My mind began to range over the map of Ireland, away from Cork city, away from Frank O'Connor and Sean O'Faolain and the man who influenced them both, Daniel Corkery, and away from Edith Somerville, County Cork's partner in that great literary combination of Somerville and Ross, away up to thoughts of Liam O'Flaherty and the storm-tossed western Aran Islands, further up to Donegal and Peadar O'Donnell's realistic and moving novel *Islanders* (1928) and across to Dromore and Omagh, Benedict Kiely country, then to the Erne countryside of Shan Bullock's *The Squireen* (1903), *Dan the Dollar* (1906) and *The Loughsiders* (1924). And after that away from Forrest Reid's *Peter Waring* (1937), his well-known rewritten portrayal of adolescence, to his less well known realistic fiction, *The Kingdom of Twilight* (1904) and *At the Door of the Gate* (1915) with its harsh portrayal of working class Belfast. Michael McLaverty's *Call My Brother Back* (1939) has pictured the rural area of the north-east with its grinding poverty as the industrial city of Belfast grew, and the depopulated land seemed blighted. And realism informs that undervalued comic novelist – and supporter of the Gaelic League – George A. Birmingham whose serious political novels include *The Seething Pot* (1905) and *The Red Hand of Ulster* (1912). *Red,* I thought. The stop sign. Is there an amber left? The whimsey of James Stephens's *The Crock of Gold* (1912) at once glowed warmly, an image of bright sunlight on the golden flowers and the green gorse bushes of the Dublin mountains. But how very different Stephens's bleaker picture of Dublin in *The Charwoman's Daughter* (1912) where the charwoman had to send her daughter out to work. And she saw the failure which this work meant, the expanding of the her daughter's life-ripples to a bleak and miserable horizon where the clouds were soap-suds and floor-cloths, and the beyond a blank resignation only made energetic by hunger. Mrs Makebelieve, rightly named, wants to keep her daughter Mary out of the world. Unrealistically. But Mrs Cafferty, mother of six, the Makebelieves' neighbour, a comic figure, reminds us of the realities of life: 'An infant and a fireplace act upon each other like magnets; a small boy is always trying to eat a kettle or a piece of coal or the backbone of a herring; a little girl and a slop-bucket are in immediate contact; the baby has a knife in its mouth; the twin is on the point of swallowing a marble, or is trying to wash itself in the butter, or the cat is about to take a nap on its face.'[2] Despite the irony – and, at times, the romance – in this novel, what remains in the reader's mind is Stephens's realistic attack on what he thought the only 'grave and debasing vice in the world – poverty'. But there are other vices that the realistic novelists have portrayed. Do you remember the dark black qualities of Brinsley

MacNamara's notorious novel, *The Valley of The Squinting Windows* (1918)? Its bitter portrayal of provincial narrowness had the terrifying quality I found in some of Carleton's stories when I was a child.

But to the present; even leaving out Moore and Joyce, I had been given a shuffled pack of cards, only there were far more than fifty-two novels in the pack, even more than 52 novelists, come to that. And more to it than recognising the aces, kings, queens, jacks and jackeens. How was one to arrange them patiently, in a game of patience where black clubs become green shamrocks, black spades bog-stained loys? But realism called, and I reached for the reference books for precise dates, to see if there was a pattern of decades, of rosaries and anti-rosaries, of pre-war and post-war repetitions, and perhaps the three-card-trick of class: big house, cottage and semi, or a trumping the ace of Westminster rule by Dublin or Belfast rule, or a shift from land hunger to sexual hunger, or a move from milk-and-white maidens to archetypally menacing Maeves and demanding Deirdres.

Enough, enough. Apart from Moore and Joyce should any other realist novelist besides Gerald O'Donovan be considered to exist before the nineteen-twenties? Gradually the subject seemed to be the realist novel *between* the wars. O'Donovan, however, came of a pre-war liberal generation that had hoped for improvement in the second decade of our century. Born Jeremiah O'Donovan, he became a priest and was an enlightened administrator in Loughrea, gaining for the new cathedral there the work of Irish artists – Sarah Purser and Jack Yeats – bringing John MacCormack to sing there, and the Irish National Theatre also to act before a large audience. O'Donovan was in favour of modernism, and refused to submit to the Papal encyclical against it of 1909, which he condemned with a cool analytic anger in his first novel *Father Ralph*, published in 1913. The world O'Donovan creates is that of small-town Ireland, that of the bourgeoisie, fast developing, and expanding in influence. And his second realistic novel, *Waiting* of 1914, tackled the problems raised for mixed marriages in Ireland by the *Ne Temere* Papal decree of 1904. He tried his hand at the political situation in *Conquest*, published in 1920, but in this novel, which ends with the

British suppression of the Dáil in 1919, the conversations too often turn into debates, and the flow of the narrative suffers as a result.

If O'Donovan's novels capture superbly the atmosphere of the Irish small town in the period before 1914, then Daniel Corkery's *A Munster Twilight* (1916) and *The Threshold of Quiet* (1917) reflect something rather different. Theirs is the world of what has been called 'puritanism and local self-satisfaction', for the urban Corkery remained a puritanical provincial. There are limits in *The Hounds of Banba* (1920) that reveal his moving away from creative literature into the literary criticism, politically – indeed almost racially – slanted, for which he is now best known. But at its best his fiction could be atmospheric, evocative and melancholic.

Corkery, however, is a pre-revolutionary figure, one of those who kept revolutionary traditions going, who helped to set the fire of 1916. What of the crucial shifts in Irish life which created the subject matter of the realist novel after 1916, between the two world wars? Joyce had left Dublin for a life of exile in 1904, and O'Donovan left Loughrea and the priesthood for his exile that same year. In doing so he provided George Moore, himself to leave Dublin six years later, with some of the subject matter for that carefully observed and psychologically persuasive experimental novel, *The Lake*.

When Moore wrote the realistic stories of *The Untilled Field* of 1903 he was portraying the after-effects of the appalling mid-nineteenth century famine, when emigration was a more effective answer to rural poverty than, for instance, the no doubt well-meant but often ill-directed efforts of the Congested Districts Board in the west of Ireland. And emigration was also an answer to the power of the priests, which Moore attacked. Influenced by Zola, parallel to Turgenev, he set down the markers for some subsequent fiction in stories such as 'Julia Cahill's Curse' and 'The Exile', which reflect the Jansenist puritanism which shaped much rural life after the famine. More striking than the negative effects of the famine, however, were those of the Wyndham Land Act of 1903 which effectively turned Ireland into a land of small farmers. Its results were that the large estate was replaced by the small farm, the big house by the small town or the streets of the expanding city.

Realistic fiction mirrored this crucial change. Maria
Edgeworth's *Castle Rackrent,* (1800) scrupulously realistic in
its speech and its facts, a story of disintegration, tells of the
decay and collapse of the big house and the landlords who
inhabited it in the 1780s. But the big house has continued to
decay and collapse ever since, with wonderful results in
realistic fiction: novels with a vertical stretch of society from
gentry to peasantry, peasantry to gentry. Generated out of
these tensions came the under-rated, indeed largely un-read,
novels of Charles Lever, the later ones in which he depicted
so realistically the decline of the landlords in the nineteenth
century, their failure of nerve, their inability to recognise
political realities. George ·Moore then pursued the theme
further with equally savage satire of the administration in
Dublin Castle in *A Drama in Muslin* (1887). The impermanence
of the big house, the great estate, and the landlords as a
cohesive class, a political force, is there also in that great
achievement of Somerville and Ross, *The Real Charlotte*
(1894). This novel, however, showed the way society was
going, for it was no longer just the story of landlord and
tenants, but of a snobbish, stratified society. Somerville and
Ross carried Maria Edgeworth's observation and realism into
twentieth-century fiction. They observed the countryside
closely, drew it lovingly in the magnificently atmospheric
descriptions of *The Real Charlotte* and their other novels. They
also recorded tellingly the nuances of speech; their differing
kinds – and classes – of people speak and behave convincingly,
and this realistic technique was at Edith Somerville's disposal
when she wrote *The Big House at Inver* in 1925. This is a
powerful, sombre attempt to capture a theme suggested much
earlier to Martin Ross by a visit to Tyrone House, where, in
her words, there had rioted three or four generations, 'living
with the countrywomen, occasionally marrying them, all
illegitimate four times over.'³ This novel was published in
1925, thirty-one years after *The Real Charlotte,* a century and
a quarter after *Castle Rackrent,* – which itself had been followed
by the other realistic Irish novels of Maria Edgeworth – *Ennui,
The Absentee* and *Ormond.* And the theme continued to occupy
Irish writers. Seumas O'Kelly in *The Lady of Deerpark* (1917),

for instance, created a novel in which realism portrays such events as the suicide of the owner so succinctly and effectively in its opening pages as to set the tone of the rest of the story with a precise particularity, marred only by an unconvincing ending. Pádraic Colum's *Castle Conquer* took up the theme of the big house in 1923; but the theme alters as time moves on. Elizabeth Bowen's *The Last September* of 1929, for instance, evokes the somewhat sinister atmosphere of a big house, its inhabitants surrounded by a countryside alive with people, still mysterious after centuries of propinquity. Here is a vignette from it of the undertones of the impending troubles. Lois, the young girl in the house, walks towards the woods where, the rumour is, someone has been seen burying guns. She is alone. Nobody wants to be involved; indeed nobody really wants to know. 'First, she did not hear footsteps coming, and as she began to notice the displaced darkness thought what she dreaded was coming, was there within her – she was indeed clairvoyant, exposed to horror and going to see a ghost. Then steps, hard on the smooth earth; branches slipped against a trench-coat. The trench-coat rustled across the path ahead, to the swing of a steady walker. She stood by the holly immovable, blotted out in her black, and there passed within reach of her hand, with the rise and fall of the stride, a resolute profile, powerful as a thought.'[4]

The impermanence of the settler in the landscape is there, as it was in Maria Edgeworth, and in the later Charles Lever, and in Somerville and Ross and in George Moore. Lois thinks: 'It must be because of Ireland he was in a hurry; down from the mountains, making a short cut through their demesne. Here was something else she could not share. She could not conceive of her country emotionally: it was a way of living, an abstract of several landscapes, or an oblique frayed island, moored at the north but with an air of being detached and washed out west from the British coast.'[5] What had happened? Elizabeth Bowen's answer is succinct: 'A man in a trench-coat passed without seeing her: that was what it had amounted to.' Less full of foreboding was Joyce Cary in *Castle Corner* (1938) but he, like Elizabeth Bowen, tempered his realism with romance, or rather was pulled each way by the two impulses. His *A House of Children* (1941) is a better, more realistic picture of ideal, timeless childhood days spent in Donegal. And the decay of the big house continues in our own time with Aidan Higgins's powerful novel *Langrishe Go Down* (1961) and Jennifer Johnston's masterly, very realistic evocations of the melancholia of disintegration and decay in *The Captains and the Kings* (1972) and *The Gates* (1973).

These novels, however, are themselves survivals of the theme of the survivors in the big house. What happened to the realistic novel between the wars was a reflection of the new, changed Ireland. The vertical range of society gives way to the horizontal – parallels with the drama are there, for Yeats's imaginative heroic plays gave way to realistic cottage comedies, with Synge's great art mediating between tragedy and comedy, between imagination and reality. Realistic novelists turned to the individual character as Ireland moved into a middle society. After the acquisition of the land what could follow? Acquisition of wealth, of social standing, made marriages, enforced respectability. Individuals could serve the despotism of an ambitious father while waiting to inherit, could conform to a society moulded by an often repressive clergy. The choice could lie between conformity or emigration to individualistic freedom. This is how Moore had seen it and how many later realistic novelists were also to interpret it after the establishment of the Irish Free State.

The way that the state came into being was, however, not convincingly treated at first. Writers were too close to it. Eimar O'Duffy in *The Wasted Island* of 1919 was over-ambitious in his picture, and, as in Gerald O'Donovan's *Conquest* of 1920, there is too much debating. Darrell Figgis in *The House of Success* (1922) was perhaps too satirical, while Liam O'Flaherty's *Insurrection* of 1950 is too fragmentary, and succumbs too much to over-melodramatic handling to be fully realistic. Iris Murdoch has recently tried her hand at it in *The Red and the Green* in 1965 but this centres too much on the characters involved. Michael Farrell's *Thy Tears May Cease* (1963), however, is a deeply personal and moving blend of realism and romance which probably captures the essence of the period better than any other novel.

After the civil war came a virtually inevitable disil-lusionment. To some realistic writers the fight for a republic had ended, in total defeat; defeat by a combination of 'an acquisitive middle class and a vigorous and uncultivated church'.[6] These are the words of John Whelan, a pupil of Daniel Corkery; another pupil, Michael O'Donovan, and he were, as the writers we know as Sean O'Faolain and Frank O'Connor, to present Ireland with a forceful picture of itself. Idealism was indeed over. The mythology of the heroic past called into fresh life in the period of the Revival, however much it had inspired the leaders of 1916, was no longer adequate for an age where there was a steady shift from country to city. This was an age when rebellion – many of the authors of the 1920s and 1930s had taken part in the actual fighting – rebellion on behalf of nationalism and its ideals turned to rebellion against the state which that nationalism had brought into being. This new state, this new Irish society seemed to the writers, particularly the realistic novelists, to threaten the restriction of the individual's development. It was certainly one which showed its dislike of those who had fought to bring it into being by banning their writing.

O'Faolain's *Bird Alone* (1936) conveys this post-independence struggle, this querying of assumptions of the realistic novelists. In it Corney Crone asserts his personal independence, but the society that surrounds him and Elsie Sherlock is unsympathetic, and sectarian conformity proves destructive in the end. Similar destructive forces are at work in O'Faolain's realistic stories. Restrictions upon individuals imposed by social and religious attitudes continue to occupy his later work – in those superb series of short stories, more tolerant now but still sharp in their reality, their radicalism and their ability to reveal the interior ideas of individuals.

Sean O'Faolain was upset when his *Midsummer Night Madness and Other Stories* was banned in Ireland in 1932. And Frank O'Connor was too, when his *The Saint and Mary Kate,* published the same year, was also banned. This is another study of obsessive religion. Like O'Faolain, O'Connor put the material of the troubles and the civil war into fiction, and his story of the shooting of hostages, 'Guests of the Nation' shows the inhuman madness, in human terms, that possessed so many. In part it may have been a purgation of experience. But in part O'Connor was getting at the ultimate loneliness of the individual, and his realism, like O'Faolain's, retained a certain undercurrent of idealistic romance. Asked in the civil war to shoot unarmed Free State soldiers courting in Cork he refused 'because this was a basic violation of the imaginative concept of life, whether of boy's weeklies or the Irish sagas'. He added to the realism of his other Chekovian stories by conveying the sound of real men and women speaking, and as a result his narrative convinces us, sweeps us along as the story unfolds.

Liam O'Flaherty is a different kind of writer. His dynamic novels centre upon the solitary, obsessed nature of central characters. He is factual in his treatment of them; Gypo Nolan of *The Informer* (1925), and the main characters of his other novels such as *The Black Soul* (1924) or *Mr Gilhooley* (1926) or *The Assassin* (1928) or *The Puritan* (1931) or *The Martyr* (1933) are all clearly in focus. Society is a backdrop in front of which they act out their rebellions. The exception is, of course, *Famine* (1937), more a picture of the whole community under stress. *Skerrett* of 1932 deals with a feud between a teacher and a priest in Inismore, and its tension is typical, as the emotional turmoil, pent up in this quarrel, spills onto O'Flaherty's pages, violently, convincingly, menacingly. It goes back to the Gothic strain in nineteenth-century Irish fiction, to the horror of Maturin's *Melmoth the Wanderer* (1820), to some of Carleton – *The Black Prophet* (1947) or *Wild Goose Lodge* in the *Traits and Stories of the Irish Peasantry* (1830; 1833) – to Sheridan Le Fanu's *The House by the Churchyard* (1863) and *Uncle Silas* (1864), even to Somerville and Ross's *An Irish Cousin* or to Bram Stoker's *Dracula*. This Gothic element, this murmuring of melodrama, lurks beneath the realism, every bit as much as the romance of, say, Emily Lawless's nineteenth-century realistic novel *Hurrish* (1886), or Elizabeth Bowen's modern *The Last September* (1924). And the romantic element lurks there too, as idealism gone temporarily to ground, in the realistic novels of O'Connor and O'Faolain.

To return to O'Flaherty and to his early collection of short stories, such as *Spring Sowing* of 1924, is to realise how good he is at conveying the reality of the rural scenes he loved. A similar interest in the land dominated much of Patrick Kavanagh's writing about Monaghan. *Tarry Flynn* (1948) contains the essence of rural life on a small farm with all its restrictions: and yet the realism must include the dream. Tarry walks backwards up the daisied slope of Callan's Hill: 'He gazed across the valley right across to the plains of Louth, and gazing he dreamed into the past. O the thrilling daisies in the sun-baked hoof-tracks. O the wonder of the dry clay. O the mystery of Eternity. . . the heavy slumbrous time and place made him forget the sting of the thorn of a dream in his heart. Why should a man want to climb out of this anonymous happiness in the conscious day.'[7] But his sister's cry of 'Tarry, Tarry, Tarry' recalls him to reality: '"What?" he shouted down. "Come down and give us a hand to teem the pot".'[8] Yes, the dream is there, however restrictive the milieu, the routine that hems it in. This contrast of dream and reality continues in the nineteen-twenties and thirties. Mary Lavin, for instance, has understood it well. She prefers the short story, she says, but one of her two novels, *The House in Clewe Street* (1945), is a masterly, faithful picture of small town life. She focuses upon apparently irrelevant details only to incorporate them tellingly in the pattern of her analyses of bereavement, of love.

She is probably right when she argues that the short story provides a necessary curb upon the oral exuberance that swirls below the surface of the prose of those Irish writers who seek, however realistically, to tell the story. Concentrated compression pays off. Compare Frank O'Connor's novel *Dutch Interior* (1940) with, say, his stories in *My Oedipus Complex and Other Stories* (1963), or compare Sean O'Faolain's novel *A Nest of Simple Folk* (1933) with, say, his *Foreign Affairs and Other Stories* (1976) and you will probably agree with me that, however good the novels, the stories have it every time.

In general the techniques used by the realistic novelists of the nineteen-twenties and thirties were not revolutionary – Moore and Joyce had done enough innovating for the time being, perhaps – but where did the thwarted idealism go, where the mythology? Perhaps one answer is to be found in the Chinese box-like satire, the realism of the word play, in Flann O'Brien's *At Swim-Two-Birds* (1939). Sometimes one is forced to the conclusion that T. S. Eliot was right when he said, 'Mankind cannot bear very much reality', for throughout

the Irish novel and realistic short stories there seems to be a
satirising of the present through the past (and not always the
heroic past of Gaeldom either) – as in the work of Darrell
Figgis, or of Eimar O'Duffy, and more recently in that of
Benedict Kiely (notably in *A Journey to the Seven Streams*) or
in the later novels of Mervyn Wall. But picking at the itching
dry scabs of social change, or the after-effects of the violence
that ushered in modern Ireland is not wholly natural to the
Irish temperament. We cannot forget the everlasting foibles
of human nature that George A. Birmingham presents so
lightheartedly or James Stephens so quizzically or Seumas
O'Kelly so drastically in the rural humour of 'The Weaver's
Grave'. The best ultimate human realism is surely to be found
in the realistic comedy of the authors which I cannot begin to
discuss within the confines of this essay, and they are Joyce,
and Beckett, and Flann O'Brien.

5. The Historical Novel

Benedict Kiely

All novels are, to some extent, historical novels, and memory may intrude even into the curious adolescent limbo of Science Fiction. Alec Trusselby, whom George Moore invented to aid and abet him in the telling of stories, said to George Moore that the best stories were hatched out of old memories. And later, George Moore, reminding Alec of his own 'words', said that stories ripen in the mouth like apples on a sunny shelf.

George Moore is as good a place as any at which to begin a consideration of the historical novel in Ireland in this century. Frank O'Connor, who was in a good position to know, held that with us the modern short story began with George Moore in the collection *The Untilled Field,* a title chosen by Moore to indicate with gentlemanly arrogance that he considered that he was clearing scutch grass and breaking ground for the first time. O'Connor's statement and Moore's arrogance may generally stand, always provided that we remind ourselves that stories, short and long, have been told since time began, something of which Frank O'Connor and George Moore were, needless to say, quite well aware.

Now it can be held with equal certainty that our Irish modern, or contemporary, novel, or the novel in relation to Irish life within our own memory and experience, begins with George Moore in *The Lake,* and in *A Drama in Muslin.* The careful reader will find in Moore's *Muslin* a curious passage carefully read and later parodied and, perhaps, surpassed by a curious writer by the name of Joyce. The passage has to do with falling snow and life and death, and the making of a journey.

But when Moore stepped back into the past he, like those heavily accoutred acrobats floundering about on the moon, took a giant step. Except that he stepped with elegance and not into nothingness nor the ashpit to which scientists have reduced that orbed maiden with white fire laden, but back

over the crowded centuries to the spring of 1614 when the
young Frenchwoman Louise Chastel, mistress of Richard de
Burgo, second Earl of Ulster, caught a chill when fishing on
Lough Corrib, and died, and was buried in Ballinrobe.

The period of the wars of Edward Bruce might seem to be
too remote to be made credible or readable about. And many
historical novelists have become such dedicated antiquarians
that they have sunk under the weight of table-tombstones.
Scott was a great man but a bad example, as witness, say
Gerald Griffin in *The Invasion,* though not in *The Duke of
Monmouth.* But Moore's feeling for the things that do not
change, in the heart or in history, meant that he could step
back over six centuries, give us the feeling of the place and
people as they must have been then and, without dissonance
or offence, make it all as alive as the morning news and
frequently more credible.

The novel I refer to is, 'Ulick and Soracha', which we will
find most conveniently where it is dovetailed, with
incomparable skill, into the second volume, mottled backed
edition, of that miracle of the later style of Moore at his most
melodic, *A Storyteller's Holiday.* His joyous book, as borrowing a notion and an adjective from Balzac, he liked to
think.

Ulick is the bastard son of that Earl Richard de Burgo, and
Louise Chastel. With his father's blessing, such as it is, Ulick,
accompanied by the harper, Tadgh Ó Dorachy, sets off for
his mother's native land to wander from castle to castle and
live the life of a *trouvère.* Young George Moore went to Paris
to try to be a painter. There are moments in which the careful
narrative reads as if it were a tale told by a man awaking from
a dream of his own ancestry. The illness that afflicts Ulick at
Dunmore, in the course of his journey to France, could have
its relation to the illness that killed John Moore, first president,
under Humbert, of the Republic of Connacht, and also the
last such president.

In faraway France a portrait painter who has been to Ireland
on a commission displays to Ulick the portraits of the three
beautiful daughters of King Ó McLaghlin of Lough Ennell,
of the family, we may assume, which had earlier in our history
sent Turguesuis the Dane, in a sort of Judith and Holofernes

story, to a watery tomb in the neighbouring lake. With one of the three faces Ulick, as a *trouvère* should, falls in love and decides to go back to Ireland and be practical about it, as many *trouvères* wisely did not, it being in those days a far more sensible course simply to sing your love.

There is one severe problem: the beloved one has already entered a convent. But she, having heard about Ulick from the painter, is restive in her vocation and anyway, George Moore had elsewhere displayed in his writings that, for some reason never as far as I know accounted for, he had a thing about rescuing nuns from convents, provided only that they were young and beautiful. Let Austin or Ulick or George have his kink to him reserved. Moore displayed that thing to unconsciously comic effect in a celebrated passage in *Memoirs of My Dead Life*.

So Ulick and Tadgh, the harper, return to a wartorn Ireland. The young nun is, so to speak, sprung. And there and then begins a beautiful and tragic love story and parallel to it, even surpassing it in living interest, the story of the wanderings of the harper through a wild afforested Ireland in the company only of a Scottish goose. An odd fragment indeed for which to reach back into the past. In a cunning key-passage in the novel Moore and his creation Alec Trusselby, the old storyteller, discuss the progress of the narration and for all sensible purposes the whole true nature of the historical novel.

But have you no fault to find, Alec, with the story so far as it's gone? Faith, I have, a fault and a half. We are mostly through the story without coming to a battle: not a word about the battle of Connor nor of the eighteen battles that the great Bruce won in the south and that made up for the beating of Felim O'Connor at Athenry. My uncle used to talk a lot of that battle, he had it all in his eye: but he hadn't got your honour's words to tell of the poor fellows tumbling over the dead, or limping off with an arrow in the thigh, with a horse shot through the nostrils screaming with pain, trampling on all in his mad way, poor beast. Sure it is as plain to me as if the battle was there in front of me. The cheering at every good shot, and the poor Irish coming on and on in their saffron tunics. The battle was fought in August when the days were long, and I can see the English coming down the hill in the after-glow, sticking and chopping about amid the blind and the lame. I'd like to have heard your honour tell of all that, but not a word, or the wind of one! Another thing is that you don't tell of the retreat of the Scots through snowstorms with troops of starving wolves on their heels eating the dead, aye, and the dying too. But, Alec, I'm not writing the history of the Bruces in Ireland. I know that, your honour, but I've been wondering if the history couldn't be mixed up in some such a way with the story that the reader wouldn't know which he was reading, but would just take it all in, and separate it all out, afterwards, in his mind. . . one thing more I'd say, I'd have Edward Bruce the hero of the story, for a finer captain never walked the world. I see, Alec, you'd have liked history better than a story: I'm sorry. It's like bread and butter they are better together, and so I'd have liked both the history and the story. But perhaps your honour is right, maybe the two wouldn't mix.[1]

Moore's subtle theorising came out of a long struggle and experience, with the history of Héloïse and Abélard, and of Greece in the time of Pericles in *Aphrodite in Aulis,* and of the Lord himself and that theory of no resurrection, no death even but a cataleptic trance, in, *The Brook Kerith.* For it is by no means necessary as we shall see later, that an Irish historical novelist should struggle only with the history of his own hapless island.

It is interesting and helpful that one of the two most notable Irish historical novels of our time should have been written by an Irish-American who long before he first set foot on the sacred soil – and that was about thirty or so years ago – was already an accomplished scholar in Irish history and literature. When Thomas Flanagan's *The Year of the French* appeared, an old friend and journalistic colleague, now deceased, asked me if this was a case of another American searching for his roots. Glad I was to be able to set him right, to explain that, from his first cognisant moment, Flanagan was, because of his parents and a most unforgettable grandmother, well aware of his roots, and that the rest was accounted for by his phenomenal reading and a final polishing with some good companions around the roads of Ireland.

We hear so much nonsense now about researching (a most dreadful participle!) a novel, even about researching a poem. In the case of this novel the novelist's life was the research and the only investigation he had specially to do was to check up a few French names and references. The book is a profound meditation on the nature of history and the elusiveness of the true nature of the past. We already know only that we cannot make much of a fist of comprehending the present. At the end of the novel Seán MacKenna, a schoolmaster and draper in Castlebar, comes back to Castlebar from Killala where he has been to collect some linen from Johnston of Sligo and, as he re-enters his own town, he tries to sort out in his mind the things that have happened there since the French sailed in.

> As I rode past Stoballs Hill in the darkness, I attempted to imagine what the great battle there had been like, the drums and bright-banners and cannon-shot and shouting. I could not. I told myself that the battle already lay with the Norman keep on the far shore of that sea which separates past from present. But that is not true, there is no such sea, it is but a trick of speech. All is bound together under God, mountain and bog, the shattered fortress and the grassy pasturelands of death, the drover's eagle that took wing upon the eve of the battle, memory, history, and fable. A trick of speech and of the blackness of night, when we are separated from one another and from the visible world. It is in the brightness of the morning air, as the poets tell us, that hope and memory walk towards us across meadows, radiant as a girl in her first beauty.[2]

Perhaps the brightest thing that Flanagan did in the building-up of this considerable book was to invent the character of the Reverend Vincent Broome of Killala and to substitute him for Bishop Stock who, as we all know, was there when the French landed and who kept a journal. A foolish consistency, Emerson said, is the hobgoblin of little minds, and to the absolutely literal minded that invention would seem to be a mere tampering with the truth of history. But if the historical novelist were not permitted the taking of such liberties then there would be no historical novels, or as George and/or Alec decided you would have all history and no story.

The trouble with Bishop Stock is that he is limited and as immoveable, it is impossible to avoid saying, as a stock or a stone. To attempt to move him would be to do even more violence to history. But Broome is as free as the novelist wishes to make him, free to go over to London, to meet and comment on the Great Lord, the eye of the whirlwind; free to comment on himself and others, on the nature of the novelist's theme, and, slyly and humorously, on the novelist himself. To Broome is given the profoundest passage in the book when he ranges in one sweep from the ragbag army of Killala to the classical style and imagination of Edward Gibbon.

Broome had once asked a learned and sagacious friend if man learned anything from history (the friend's name was not, as far as I know, Hegel), and the friend told him that you did not learn anything from history, but is was possible to learn from historians. To this matter, while reading the capacious works of Hume and Gibbon, he had given much thought. Then Flanagan-Broome, or Broome-Flanagan writes:

> Gibbon gives to us the breadth of the classical world from the Hellespont to the Pillars of Hercules, a vast temple with colonnades and recesses, glowing white marble beneath a blazing Mediterranean sun, and displays to us then its hideous and shameful destruction. How firm a sense do we derive of all its constituent parts, of their intricate relationships. How certain is its destruction, with alien creeds subverting its powers and alien races wearing away its far-flung frontiers. Each cause and reason is locked securely into place. And, over all the mighty drama presides the awesome authority of Gibbon's splendid language, his unimpassioned rationality. Here, we think, is the chief civil drama of human history, in which tens and hundreds played their parts, but drama compelled by the human mind to yield up its uttermost secrets. Great was Rome and catastrophic was its fall, but great too is the energy of the historian's mind, the cool deliberation of his judgment.[3]

But then afterthoughts come to the Reverend Mr Broome,

the self-satirising Gibbon of Killala. Perhaps it has not been at all as Edward Gibbon had described it. Perhaps everything had been chaos, chance, ill-luck or simply the judgment of God, as had in more pious ages been believed. Perhaps everything that he had read had been only Gibbon's imagination: 'And the past remains therefore unknowable, shrouded in shadow, an appalling sprawl of buildings, dead men, battles, unconnected, mute, half-recorded. Perhaps we learn nothing from history and the historian teaches only that we are ignorant.'⁴ And on Irish history in particular he has this mournful reflection.

> How many dramas of modern history have chosen for setting this God-forsaken bog, and always without any recompense for my unfortunate countrymen save further misery. What were the rebellions of Desmond and Tyrone but chapters in the struggle between Elizabeth and Spain and thus of Reformation and Counter-Reformation? What were the wars of Cromwell here but a sideshow to the English Civil War, in which the divine right of kings was challenged and overthrown? When James and William, the two kings, faced each other at the Boyne, the game was Europe, and Ireland was but a board upon which the wagers were placed.
>
> The history of Ireland, as written by any of our local savants, reminds me of a learned and be-spectacled ant climbing laborously across a graven tablet and discovering there deep valleys, towering mountains, broad avenues, which to a grown man contemplating the scene are but the incised names of England, Spain, France. Now the name of France appears a second time upon the tablet.⁵

That last passage quoted represents an elegant and cynical point of view and it is given in the novel to George Moore of Moore Hall, grand-uncle of the novelist, man-about-London, and country-gentleman who spent his life writing, most appropriately, a history of the Girondins which, also most appropriately, was never to be published. From what we know, mostly through George Moore the novelist, about George Moore the unpublished historian, it seems certain that he would have thought and written exactly like that, and on the part of Flanagan that was another neat piece of guessing about the nature of the past.

For the historical novel can be, for good or bad, many things: an escape from the present into an imagined past; or a genuine attempt to study the past; or a study of human nature in a setting of the past and with relevance to our own time; or a putative study of the nature of history and, thus, also with relevance to our own time; or a clearer viewing of a present problem against a background of the past; or all in together. And more besides. Between, say, George Moore and John Banville in the historical novel as written by Irishmen in this century you may, if you care to, study most of the varieties.

A list of some eighteen names, possibly not complete and not including the three already mentioned occurs to me: Francis MacManus, Joseph O'Neill, Maurice Walsh, Thomas Kilroy, Kate O'Brien, James Plunkett, Liam O'Flaherty, Eimar O'Duffy, Philip Rooney, Donn Byrne, Michael Farrell, Conal O'Riordan, Austin Clarke, Francis Stuart, George A. Birmingham, Eilis Dillon, Canon Sheehan, W. F. Marshall. Ample matter for the research student who has time and space at his or her command.

To demonstrate the differences and the resemblances between the history and the story we can do no better than turn to Eimar O'Duffy's novel *The Lion and the Fox*, the fox of the title being Florence MacCarthy Mór whose complicated character, for which the circumstances of the time were not perhaps entirely responsible, is described in remarkable detail.

About him it was said there were as many different opinions as there were men who knew him. He was a courtier at Elizabeth's Windsor, an Irish chieftain in Munster, a lawyer in the law-courts and everywhere, because he was exceedingly tall and handsome, the cynosure of all eyes. The English mistrusted him for a rebel. The Irish believed him in league with the English. He was high in favour with Queen Elizabeth, sworn brother to Sir Thomas Norreys and the very idol of the people of Munster. But by address and cunning he committed himself irrevocably to neither side so that it was impossible to tell whether he was holding Munster for the Queen or plotting its liberation.

The speaker in O'Duffy's novel made a good effort to sum-up things that defied summation, or to clarify something that seemed only to become more obscured by the accumulation of detail. What he was really adumbrating were the tricks and prudencies and smiles and evasions that an Irish gentleman/ chieftain at that time, and particularly a man so important as the MacCarthy Mór, had to practice in order to survive.

We can be pretty certain that Eimar O'Duffy had read *The Life and Letters of Florence MacCarthy Reagh, Tanist of Carbery, MacCarthy Mór,* with some Portion of the History of the Ancient Families of the South of Ireland, Compiled Solely from Unpublished Documents in Her Majesty's State Paper Office by Daniel MacCarthy Glas, of Gleann a Chroim. That enormous book was published in the Fenian year of 1867 by Longmans in London and Hodges and Smith in Dublin; and in 1975 it was photocopied and republished by the Miros Press in Cork. More than anything I have ever read it enables the reader to live in those times, to see the people and the places, to listen to and think with the people. It was a gift from the gods to the historical novelist, and to the student of the historical novel it now provides an unique opportunity to balance the novel against the source, just as one can do with *The Old Yellow Book* that Robert Browning stumbled on among the rubble and out of which he fashioned that great historical novel *The Ring and The Book.*

The author of *Pacata Hibernia,* that Thomas Stafford who was the adulator of and possibly the ghost-writer for Thomas Carew, Queen's President of Munster, was in no doubt as to the character of Florence. 'It would be too tedious to set down at large the manifest proofs of Florence's juggling treasons; wherefore I will, for brevity's sake, relate but a few more abstracts of letters and examinations which here ensue.'[6] And Standish James O'Grady, in his editing of *Pacata Hibernia* and from a very different point of view than that held by the complacent author of that text, said: 'Had this chief played a bold straight part he should have been able to beat Carew without any assistance from anyone.'[7] And: 'Had Florence been true to Tyrone Irish history might have been different. Had he been true to the crown he would have lived and flourished as the Earl of Clancarty and the greatest nobleman in Ireland.'[8]

There is, though, another less simple way of looking at it. Florence MacCarthy may have groaned, as the novelist sees him, with the instinctive knowledge of the man who saw both sides too clearly. Which of us now is to say what he really thought of O'Neill or how he, Florence, would have viewed his own prospects if O'Neill were to become complete Lord of the Gael. Perhaps there were moments when there seemed to be little difference between the wiles of my Lord Cecil in London and the wiles of the great Earl in the black mountains of the North. We, and Standish O'Grady, employ a hindsight given to us by an Irish nationalism that, to judge by some of its end-products in our own time, may not exactly have been perfection to begin with.

The large work of Daniel MacCarthy Glas would seem to indicate something of the sort. It echoes the very voices of the time and can, indeed, be read as if it *were* a most exciting historical novel, as *Pacata Hibernia* cannot. Standish O'Grady did point out that it was possible to think that the complacent author of *Pacata* might have been a blind man '. . . so little does he tell us of the things we really desire to know. . . so one may travel for hours through the state papers without getting one glimpse of the men of whom they treat.'[9]

A good novelist or an historian with the ability to write can breathe life into such dry bones. It was greatly to the credit of Eimar O'Duffy that with such splendid original material at his disposal he in no way diminished it when he produced the novel, as has happened in other cases. Consider, for instance, A. E. W. Mason's novel *Clementina* and how it loses by comparison with the original story of the great adventure of the Chevalier Wogan as told straight by J. M. Flood in *The Life of Chevalier Charles Wogan*.[10]

In striking contrast with the plenitude of material that O'Duffy had at his disposal are the slender sources on which Francis MacManus built up the most notable historical novel written by an Irishman in our times, the trilogy *Stand and Give Challenge, Candle for the Proud,* and *Men Withering,* which we may accept as one novel. Or were the sources really so slender: a handful of poems, a headful of folklore, a scholar's knowledge of the century in which the poet lived. There can be even in one poem a world of information and inspiration. MacManus, himself, beginning the work when he was a young fellow of twenty-five, stated his case in a way that has wise and general application to the nature of the historical novel:

> This book may send shivers of pedantic disapproval up and down the spines of historians and biographers. It is not an essay in history of which I have been very sparing; still less an essay in biography of which we possess but rags and tatters; and again still less an essay in Gaelic literary criticism. It is an attempt to present the lives of a few people, as I have conceived them, of the hidden Ireland. You and I, had we been alive and Irish and troubled with song, might have been such a person as the chief character who lived when a dark nightmare was on this nation."[11]

The young, rebellious poet in the early pages of the trilogy may or may not be historical. He is undoubtedly a twentieth-century democrat's projection of himself into another century when a broken people had accepted helotry and their poets gave them coloured dreams about a Stuart king. We can know so little about the realities of that time. The redheaded poet's meditation on the people, as he walked from the Samhain fair at Cappoquin, could scarcely have burdened the minds of many of the school of poets spinning fancies about wandering hawks and Caesars over the sea. But they would come logically enough from a free man in a free society meditating on the spectacle of slavery at any time and in any place:

> A rift in the clouds, the moon sailed across the bared patch of sky, and there beneath the light were the ridged beloved hills, the plume-like trees – and slimy, damp, lice-infested cabins. Inside these cabins the people would be gathered on this holy night of All Souls, while the wandering spirits of the dead drifted before the purgatorial winds. They would tell stories about the dead, about Fionn and the Fianna, about the heroes and gods and philosophers of Greece, about saints and kings and princes and lovely ladies, as if no care or worry ever touched them, and on the morrow or the day afterwards they would pay their

last rents and go home to live in want or die of starvation.
Why did they yield? Why did they not fight?[12]

The poet of the trilogy loves this broken people, possibly
because he belongs to them. The novelist who wrote the
trilogy made things hard for his own heart by looking for a
long time at his own people as they were in their deepest
degradation. He spares neither himself nor the people, nor the
poet whose soul for a time is hardened by apostacy and pride,
nor the reader. Writing three novels, or one very long novel
about the poet, Donnacha Rua Mac Conmara, whose
shadowy odyssey began in the first half of the eighteenth
century and came down to days when mysterious strangers
whispered news of a new gospel in France, is as good a way
as any other for a novelist to learn discipline in style. Steady
and continuous contemplation of a degraded people is the best
possible discipline for the emotions. One result of that
discipline, as far as an Irish writer is concerned, is that it
becomes possible to accept Ireland without being sentimental
about Ireland. There can be less softness of feeling in the
acceptance displayed by MacManus than in the rejection made
classical by James Joyce and so subtly analysed by Sean
O'Faolain. The emotions in this great work are disciplined
but they are never deadened. Donnacha Rua, walking the
roads, can shorten his journey and lighten the load on his heart
in the company of spalpeens and tinkers, beggars and pedlars.
'Whenever he wearied of voices and faces he drank deeply of
the loveliness of the land about him. At times he spoke aloud
the beginning of his new song and added lines to it: and then
he moved as in a sleep.'[13]

The second MacManus novel, *The Greatest of These*, raises
an interesting general point. It tells the story of a rebellious
priest who has withdrawn into a mountain solitude and of the
search for him by a bishop to whom he had, in happier times,
been tutor and inspiration. The story, or the original from
which it grew, would have been still alive in the memory of
people in the Kilkenny countryside when MacManus was a
young man. So that one cannot say that the novelist was
stepping back into history but moving rather in that shadowy
territory well known to the Reverend Vincent Broome, where

past and present mingle, and where we will also find Liam O'Flaherty's trilogy, *Famine, Land* and *Insurrection.*

Perhaps the most notable novel to be found in that half-lighted world would be Thomas Kilroy's *The Big Chapel.* There were literary dangers in trying to do what Kilroy did in that book: to take a story out of the immediate and almost tangible past, in that case a particularly agonising one, and to make it live again with contemporary intensity. But by technique and good writing and, above all, by human understanding Kilroy triumphed.

It was perhaps a mistake for the publisher's blurb to attempt to relate what happened in Callan, County Kilkenny, a hundred years ago to the bigotries and violence of our own time. Reckless readers might go searching for analogies that are not there. Except to Dr Paisley, Ultramontanism is not now our chief problem and even he does not mention it in public as much as he used to. Topicality, God bless the mark, was not what the novelist was after. He gave us a novel about passion and agony, misunderstanding and hatred at all times and in all places, and also about unswerving and pitiable love.

In the novel a priest defies his bishop and cardinal over papal infallibility and attendant matters. A town is split up into two factions. Violence and burnings follow. A story that started with stars and shepherds ends in a sort of horror. Staggering in his darkness, the man, a great tragic figure who is the centre of all this, cries out: 'Your salvation is in what you do, not what's done to you.'[14] But the balloon ascent on which, with uncanny skill, Kilroy makes the novel almost to end, comes to grief in a nearby wood with the balloonist, like Mad Sweeney, more dead than alive amid the branches, and the brief chronology that follows chills the heart. The priest dies in the County Home. The family of schoolmaster Scully, which had become involved with him, is destroyed, and disfigured even to the next and final generation. The town, or the world, goes on as always, no better, no worse.

What I have so far said may be taken as introduction to the detailed study of, I reckon, about forty novels by about twenty different hands. It would be fascinating, for instance, to study Joseph O'Neill's novel about Norse Dublin, *Wind From the*

North and to relate its method and content to his novel about Lord Essex, *Chosen By The Queen,* in which it would almost seem that the novelist had read Ben Jonson until his head echoed with the rhythm of the time. Or to delight in the comedy of Austin Clarke's *The Bright Temptation,* and to compare it with that strangest of poet's notebooks, *The Singing Men at Cashel.* Or to follow Philip Rooney with Redmond Count O'Hanlon in *North Road,* or, with the Ouzel Galley, all the way to Barbary and back in *The Golden Coast.* Or to go with Maurice Walsh on an oddly happy journey in Elizabethan or rather anti-Elizabethan Ireland in *Blackcock's Feather,* and to compare that book with one of the best of our historical novels, *And No Quarter,* in which Walsh wrote about the wars of Montrose. Or with John Banville to follow the earth round the sun in his novel on Copernicus. Banville has written also on Kepler and, even if Robert Browning was there before him, I feel he should try a tumble with Paracelsus.

'Know not for knowing's sake, but to become a star to men forever.'

6. The Autobiographical Novel

Thomas Kilroy

The first question, I suppose, has to be: what do we mean by the term autobiographical fiction?

To begin with there is, obviously, that fiction which is demonstrably based upon recorded facts in the author's own life. And there is a special kind of pleasure to be had from reading such fiction with the facts of the author's life beside us. The fiction glows with the presences behind it, numinous and lit from a source beyond the imagination. Common curiosity, the most potent drive behind all our reading of novels and biographies, is given added charge as it were. At the same time, we are made to feel a party to the process of fiction-making itself, to the way in which the writer transmutes fact into fiction. It is this kind of pleasure, and illumination, that we get from a reading of a great literary biography like that of James Joyce by Richard Ellmann. I am certainly not going to try and talk about autobiographical fiction in this highly specialised way.

Instead I have made a rather arbitrary list of Irish novels which might be said, in one way or another, to be about growing up in this country in the first half of the century. And this process so described would appear to have come out of the personal experiences of the novelists, although I am not going to try to make such connections absolute. I am going to try instead to use my list as a field of reference to say something about the way in which the autobiographical mode may shape fiction and I am going to remark upon the images of Irish life which such novels offer to us. At any rate, here are the novels, in chronological sequence:

Joyce's *A Portrait of the Artist as a Young Man*, Sean O'Faolain's *A Nest of Simple Folk*, Michael McLaverty's *Call My Brother Back*, Patrick Kavanagh's *Tarry Flynn*, Anthony C. West's *The Ferret Fancier*, Michael Farrell's *Thy Tears Might Cease*, Brian Moore's *The Emperor of Ice Cream*, and John

McGahern's *The Dark*. There is one other novel to which I
want to refer, quite different to these others, in which the
autobiographical *is* the central mode and in a highly original
way, Francis Stuart's *Black List: Section H.*

I am more interested in the inventiveness of these books
than in their fidelity to specific histories. Having said that I
must immediately qualify it. There is one idea of history that
is entirely relevant, that which is understood by the German
word *Bildung*. The primary meaning of *Bildung* is the
individual's quest or journey in pursuit of inner wholeness,
inner maturity. In the nineteenth century German aestheticians
appropriated this word in order to describe a particular kind
of novel, the *Bildungsroman,* which had at its centre the *Bildung*
of its hero, his journey towards fulfilment. The German
Bildungsroman, from Goethe to Thomas Mann answered
peculiarly German philosophical needs. It differed in emphases
from the development of similar fiction in other languages.
You could hardly describe each of the novels on my list as an
example of *Bildungsroman*. Yet each shares its features and since
I am going to talk about the Irishness of the books it is as well
to acknowledge right away that they are also part of a larger,
European tradition.

We begin with Joyce's Stephen Dedalus, but one year before
the publication of *A Portrait* two other novels appeared which
help to illustrate the extensiveness of this kind of fiction. D.
H. Lawrence's *Sons and Lovers* and François Mauriac's *L'Enfant
Chargé de Chaînes (Young Man in Chains)* have at their centres,
like *A Portrait,* a young protagonist of exceptional sensitivity
undergoing the stresses and trials of growth towards
manhood. The environment, in contrast to the young man's
sensibility, is markedly philistine and in Lawrence and
Joyce this is personalised in a boorish, authoritarian father-
figure. All three heroes move within the shadow of a mother
from whom they seek independence through their own rather
anguished experimenting with sexuality. The culture within
each of the novels is heavily infused with religious
evangelicalism. Finally, each novel embodies and redefines an
idea of human freedom. Here, in however sketchy a fashion,
we have some of the essential elements of the *Bildungsroman*
as it developed away from its German source.

The talismanic word is freedom. It pervades the endings of these novels; it is the goal or grail at the end, the seal upon the young hero's coming of age, sometimes concrete, sometimes evanescent, dream-like, suspended before the hero like the image of the city before Paul Morel in Lawrence's *Sons and Lovers*. In the last few pages of *A Portrait* Stephen Dedalus ('FREE. Soul free and fancy free.')[1] escapes into that most unencumbered of all literary forms, the personal diary. There is the illusion of absolute freedom in the writing but the new exposure, the nakedness of the presentation, intensifies the irony with which Joyce has treated his hero from the beginning. For this reason, the aspirations, the mild heroics of the book's ending are peculiarly touching. Even if one did not have Joyce's other treatment of Stephen in *Ulysses* one would still respond to the pathos of Stephen's hopes at the end of *A Portrait*. Nevertheless, the choice taken is a Joycean one so that it may be said that this novel answers the chief technical challenge of autobiographical fiction: the creation of a fictional distance between author and subject while at the same time preserving the personal statement at the novel's core. Stephen rejects the turn to the past of the early Yeats in favour of a future, however unknown. It is in this sense that freedom can only have a pure meaning by way of reference to a future. The word has a rosy blush to it; it breathes with expectation; its commonest figurative image is that of a new dawn. All of this, in all its youthfulness Joyce has rendered through Stephen's apostrophe: 'Not this. Not at all. I desire to press in my arms the loveliness that has not yet come into the world.'[2] Here is the equivalent from John McGahern, half a century later in *The Dark*: 'You were walking through the rain of Galway with your father and you could laugh purely, without bitterness, for the first time, and it was a kind of happiness, at its heart the terror of an unclear recognition of the reality that set you free, touching you with as much foreboding as the sodden leaves falling in this day, or any cliché.'[3]

The direct address to the hero in this narrative is the McGahern technique to create a distance, a space between the author and his creation, and it successfully controls a book which threatens, at times, to succumb to its own anger. But the tone here is typical in its relief and fear before the implications of such relief on the threshold of adulthood. What these books catch is the pause between childhood and adulthood where absolute self-possession seems possible, thrilling and terrifying as it may be. The body of each novel has to do with the struggle towards this point, a conflict, to use Hegel's lovely phrase 'between the poetry of the heart and the resisting prose of circumstance'.

What characterises the Irish fiction is the degree of the resistence, the circumstances of Irish social life rather than the triumph of the poetic heart. It is quite extraordinary how little has changed in the lives of the young in these fifty years. Stephen Dedalus flying the nets about him, escaping from what a later Irish poet, Desmond O'Grady, was to call 'Mother Church, Mother Land and Mother', would have found the same forces persisting if he had strayed into the fiction of the later novelists. Freedom, then, in this Irish fiction has a pronounced sociological stress; the emphatic burden of Irishness, and it is not just simply of the Catholic variety, is so strong that the novels tend to submerge; little space is left for exploring human development in its essence. Freedom may even remain illusive, like the unclimbed hill of Knockbawn in Anthony C. West's *The Ferret Fancier,* a simple symbolic way of showing the sectarianism and puritanism which surround young Simon in that book.

Even in those books which appear to lift above the fear and hatred of life there is the constant reminder of the appalling human waste. In Michael McLaverty, the writer's own faith in his religion allows a peaceful resolution at the end of *Call My Brother Back.* Confessional and Christmas Crib stand as reassurances to Colm McNeill despite the wreckage visited upon his young life. But even in the acquiescence, the *pietas,* the writing conveys a profound exhaustion at the wasting of life. The boy walks along the tow-path of the Lagan beyond the horrors of Belfast. 'And all this beauty, all these quiet places flowed into his heart and filled him with a tired-torn joy.'[4] The journey back into the city is a journey back into nightmare. That night, this child-adult bolts the door against the outside and it is only in the drifting towards sleep, below the wavering light of the crib, that he is granted his vision of personal freedom. It comes out of his memories, out of a lost childhood, irretrievable and still under the oppression from outside that bolted door. 'He went up to bed, and on the landing saw the lamp burning before the crib and above it a wavering circle of light on the ceiling. In bed he lay awake, his mind swirling to and fro. . . rabbits wild and free on the hills around Belfast. . . swans moving across black water. . . oil-lamps warming the windows in Rathlin . . . a rusty tin in the fork of a thorn bush. . . a rickle of bones falling dead in York Street. . .'[5]

Patrick Kavanagh's Tarry Flynn, on the other hand, bounds into the future with the encouragement of the disreputable but philosophical uncle who has recently arrived into his life. Here is Tarry. 'He was wearing a new suit and he had a new soul, brand new, wondering at the newly created world.'[6] What puts *Tarry Flynn* apart from all these other novels is its vigorous, comic tolerance. There is a sense in which it transcends the squalor and constriction of the life it portrays. Nevertheless, it is all there, as potent as in any other of the novels: the puritanical religion, the sexual guilt, the fear and timidity before life, the narrowness of society, the fierce consuming hold of the mother and of the land, the dreams of the young crypto-artist. What lightens the book is Kavanagh's sense of fun and warm mockery with which he treats Tarry but his treatment of rural Irish life is relentless. The whole comedy, for example, is based upon the appalling statistic of Tarry's age, twenty-seven and never having kissed a girl, so that the whole novel is a parody of the novel of adolescence in which the growing-pains have been unnaturally postponed. What saves Tarry is what so often saves the protagonists of this kind of fiction: his sensitivity: 'a man who had seen the ecstatic light of life in stones, on the hills, in leaves of cabbages and weeds.'[7]

In three of the novels, those of Sean O'Faolain, Michael Farrell and Michael McLaverty, the struggle towards inner integrity is counterpoised by the struggle of Irish Nationalism, 1916, the Black and Tan War, the riven Belfast of the early 1920s. In both O'Faolain and McLaverty the rebellion of Nationalism is used as an indirect measurement of the worth of the protagonist's new maturity; the revolutionary sacrifice is made by others, an uncle, a brother, so that not only is the political theme personalised, it is reduced to a place within the true theme which is personal development. Michael Farrell's book deals with the War of Independence in a more direct fashion and his hero, Martin, is in the middle of it.

Yet even in the Farrell novel the political is absorbed into something else, a different kind of confrontation, inward-looking and quite remote from the public arena of politics and national independence. Martin may be dedicated to the IRA on the ground but within he is dedicated to what Thomas Mann called 'an individualistic cultural conscience.'[8] All these Irish books are very much preoccupied with the individual's painful attempts to hammer out a 'cultural conscience', that is, a personal morality based upon response to what is beautiful in life and beautiful in art.

Thy Tears Might Cease may give a vivid picture of the savagery on both sides in the Black and Tan War. It may end with the prison closing-in on the rebel Martin, but the climax of the book is to be found in its statement of the idea of freedom, based upon the old European radical cry of liberty, equality and fraternity. In one climactic scene in the novel, Martin confronts a professor at University College to seek a safe cover for his IRA activities. The scene clearly echoes that between Stephen and the Dean in *A Portrait:* the young rebel in an exchange of issues with the figure of authority of middle-class, Catholic, anglicised Ireland. The old antagonism of England and Ireland lies behind both scenes. But that antagonism has been borrowed, as it were. In associating Dean and professor with anglicisation, the political is being used in both novels to inscribe another kind of tyranny, the domination of the individual's consciousness. For Martin, the revolution is the hope of a freedom that will go beyond the repossession of the country. When the professor accuses him of anti-clericalism, he replies: 'Anti-clericalism? Oh, nothing so old-fashioned as that, sir. We are riddled with the hope of seeing truth and freedom at last in Ireland.'[9]

If the goal of these novels is Freedom, the form of each novel is constructed around systems of enclosure and restraint that have to be broken down or circumvented. I want to refer to two such structures, very briefly, both embedded within the European tradition of the *Bildungsroman,* both of immense importance to these Irish books as well. The first is the image of enclosure based on place, the fact that movement towards selfhood is charted, as it were, by a movement from the periphery to the centre, the provinces to the metropolis where the city stands as an image of glittering, human possibility. The second is the archetypal struggle between father and son in which the language of love and the language of hate become welded into a kind of single, grievous idiom.

The movement towards a centre is an imaginative reflection of the urbanisation of modern technological societies over the past two centuries where to be modern was to experience the metropolitan scene. The remarkable thing about the Irish fiction is the degree to which this is resisted. In part, this is due to the trauma of emigration or, indeed, migration in the Irish psyche and in part to the immensely complex feelings which most Irish writers have towards the rural landscape. Of the novels on my list, only the Joyce and Moore are thoroughly urban and without much dependence upon lyrical evocations of the countryside. While admitting that some of them are early, even first novels, it is nevertheless remarkable that the others, the O'Faolain, McLaverty, Kavanagh, West, Farrell and McGahern, draw upon the rural scene with such force, such painful intimacy, such nostalgia, that movement away, whatever the release, is always problematical.

Nothing is quite as disturbing in this fiction as the clash between parent and child. It accounts for much of the power in Brian Moore's *The Emperor of Ice Cream* and John McGahern's *The Dark* as well as the final section of the O'Faolain novel. Again this motif testifies to the deep conservatism at the centre of Irish life since the struggle is identified, in each case, as a struggle between new values and old. There is seldom the capitulation of the old as you get it at the end of Brian Moore's novel. The usual is a kind of qualified victory on the part of the young. Moore's case is interesting because although, like Joyce, he was to remain heavily dependent upon the Irish scene for his material throughout his subsequent writing career his emotional remove from it is almost surgically complete. The usual condition in these Irish novelists up to the middle of the century is more likely to be one where what has been left behind is still palpably there, what has been defeated has exacted its own form of victory.

The distinction of Francis Stuart's *Black List: Section H* from all of this is that it is a book which engages autobiography at the point, and from the perspective, of adult maturity. The journey outward of personal exploration is made from the point at which the *Bildungsroman* may traditionally be said to end. One effect of this is that the old obstacles to growth are met, not with just a mature personality but with an ideology of a deeply subversive kind. The ideology of H, Stuart's protagonist in the book, is one of romantic, radical dissent. The artist as a free explorer of all experience, including, perhaps especially, an explorer of the forbidden, the taboos of conventional society. The artist as a wise fool, a triumphant victim where success is measured by his embrace of defeat. The last lines of this novel run like this: 'Whatever it was at the other end there was no way of telling. It might be a howl of final despair or the profound silence might be broken by certain words that he didn't yet know how to listen for.'[10] It is one of the most potent, most seductive versions of freedom in literature, from Blake and Shelley to the one writer who haunts the pages of *Black List: Section H,* Dostoevski. One aspect of its power is that in making the autobiographical the central mode in writing, it effectively makes the writer himself the hero of his own imagination. The world then is reconstituted from this highly idiosyncratic point of view; no more absolute freedom is possible in this life. Part of the strange force of Stuart's book is that this expression of personal freedom is made against the unimaginable repression and tyranny of the Second World War. There is nothing fixed about this ideology since its meaning implies a continuous process of discovery. Each of these novels share in the experience of alienation from the middle ground of Irish life but Stuart's is the most extreme version of this. It is an understanding of the artistic sensibility which has its beginnings in Irish fiction in George Moore but the key text remains Joyce's *A Portrait of the Artist as a Young Man.*

Francis Stuart's book deliberately and with passionate conviction undermines the whole claim to truth of recorded facts, including the facts of autobiography. He allows the facts of his own autobiography, his marriage to Iseult Gonne, his relationship to Maud Gonne and Yeats, his own sojourn in Nazi Germay, to surface in the fiction like a skeletal frame, undisguisedly part of lived history. Nevertheless, all is fiction. The imagination plays and fabricates about this frame, this concrete factuality until it too becomes a part of the book's vision, the book's fiction. The effect is startling, the kind of triumph over the circumstances of a lived life which autobiographical fiction always strives for, freedom even in the defeat, defeat, that is, according to the world's terms, where victory is in the act of writing itself.

The claim is sometimes made that the total corpus of any imaginative writer, poet, novelist, playwright, makes up a kind of spiritual autobiography. It is in the blend of biographical fact and fictional composition, however, that the whole mystery of the creative comes into play. Writers themselves are acutely, even ironically, aware of this competitiveness in the human mind between fact and fiction. There is a wonderful interview with Patrick Kavanagh in the pages of *The Bell,* in 1948, where he compares the truth, respectively, of his novel *Tarry Flynn* and his autobiography *The Green Fool*. The novel, he claims, is 'nearer the truth' than the autobiographical record. 'I've been telling lies all my life [he said]. I invented so many stories about myself in *The Green Fool* to illustrate my own unique character that I don't know myself what's true about me and what isn't.'[11] It is a comic version of a condition which many writers will recognise as they try to marshal the past to leave a record, any record, for the future.

7. The Fiction of James Joyce

Denis Donoghue

In the fourth chapter of Joyce's *Portrait of the Artist as a Young Man*, the young man Stephen Dedalus is walking along the wooden bridge down the Bull Wall. 'He drew forth,' Joyce reports, 'a phrase from his treasure and spoke it softly to himself:

> – A day of dappled seaborne clouds.
>   The phrase and the day and the scene harmonised in a chord. Words. Was it their colours? He allowed them to glow and fade, hue after hue: sunrise gold, the russet and green of apple orchards, azure of waves, the grey-fringed fleece of clouds. No, it was not their colours: it was the poise and balance of the period itself. Did he then love the rhythmic rise and fall of words better than their associations of legend and colour? Or was it that, being as weak of sight as he was shy of mind, he drew less pleasure from the reflection of the glowing sensible world through the prism of a language many-coloured and richly storied than from the contemplation of an inner world of individual emotions mirrored perfectly in a lucid supple periodic prose?'[1]

The part of his treasure from which Stephen has drawn the phrase – a day of dappled seaborne clouds – is a book by a minor early nineteenth-century American writer, Hugh Miller, called *The Testimony of Rocks; or, Geology in its Bearings on the Two Theologies, Natural and Revealed;* it was published in 1857. The book is an attempt to reconcile the biblical account of creation with the new arguments from geology. At one point far out in the book, Miller imagines Satan contemplating the divine creation but unable to comprehend it; least of all to comprehend that God has created the universe as a home, Miller says, for 'higher and higher forms of existence'. How must Satan have felt, he says, 'when looking back upon myriads of ages, and when calling up in memory what once had been, the features of the earth seemed scarce more fixed to his view than the features of the sky in a day of dappled, breeze-borne clouds. . .'[2]

You'll notice that Stephen has not recalled the phrase quite accurately: 'breeze-borne' has become 'sea-borne'. But no matter. What is more to the point is that the phrase has floated free from its context and lodged in his mind as an independent particle of language, as if it were a phrase in music, which in a sense it is. Stephen is not averse to satanic contemplation, but it is the phrase as such that has occurred to him, not even the sentence in which it has participated.

When Stephen starts questioning himself about his relation to words, he comes upon several possibilities, but mostly to dispose of them. The colours of words: it was a standard speculation, especially in nineteenth-century French poetry and poetics, that syllables might be related to one another as in the relation of colours, shades, and tones; that the syllables of a word might stir into action the several senses, and not merely the mind intent on replacing the word by its meaning. Stephen puts aside the notion, at least for the moment, and he thinks of his preference for the rhythmic rise and fall of words rather than 'their associations of legend and colour'. I have always interpreted that phrase as pointing to the early Yeats, and to his cult of what Ezra Pound called 'the associations that hang near words'. If so, Stephen's preference is an occasion, one of many, on which Joyce distanced himself from a Yeatsian aesthetic which he had to guard himself against, as against an exotic temptation.

The third possibility Stephen considers is the most telling one; that he derives less pleasure from 'the glowing sensible world' reflected in language than from 'an inner world of individual emotions mirrored perfectly in a lucid supple periodic prose'. It is itself a glowing preference, but a curious one. The sensible world glows and is sensible only to a mind interested in seeing it in that character; interested to the point of seeing it 'through the prism of a language many-coloured and richly storied'. There is no question of merely seeing the world as in itself, severely, it really is. We are free to think that Stephen, short-sighted or not, sees the glow of the world

enough to be afraid of seeing it too keenly; as if he were afraid
that the 'inner world' of his purely individual emotions might
have to take a secondary place in his sensibility. So he moves
from the colours of language, its glows and associations, to
whatever quality is enacted in 'a lucid supple periodic prose'.

It sounds as if he means a style chiefly characterised by its
syntax, and means to praise the flexibility of its performances;
which is very odd, since the phrase which started the whole
speculation has no syntax at all and is all poetic diction. But
I think Stephen is urging himself to move beyond the rich
adhering words of a poetic diction – to escape from his lyric
prison, to a life of decision and action, much as Yeats had to
put behind him the entrancing associations that hang near
words before he could write the far more resilient poems of
his middle books.

How much Stephen has to urge himself to leave the lyric
prison is shown on the next page, his mind still occupied by
Miller's phrase, 'Disheartened, he raised his eyes towards the
slow-drifting clouds, dappled and seaborne. They were
voyaging across the deserts of the sky, a host of nomads on
the march, voyaging high over Ireland, westward bound. The
Europe they had come from lay out there beyond the Irish
Sea, Europe of strange tongues and valleyed and woodbegirt
and citadelled and of entrenched and marshalled races.'[3]

That is not a style in which a writer goes forth to do
anything. Stephen's diction is drawn from literature, from
anthologies of prose style, and diverse translations of Latin,
Greek and German texts. But I would make much of his sense
of Europe, which extends, a few pages later, into more
particular affiliations; references to the plays of Gerhart
Hauptmann, Newman's prose, 'the dark humour of Guido
Cavalcanti', 'the spirit of Ibsen', and a line of poetry recalled
from Ben Jonson.

I have gone into the episode in the *Portrait* mainly to
emphasise that to Joyce, as to Stephen, language always
seemed to offer itself as a counter-truth to the truth of reality.
Of course, among his many senses of language he had a
journeyman's sense, too. He was quite willing to treat
sentences as useful instruments to disclose a reality not itself
linguistic. One of the stories in *Dubliners* begins: 'Mrs Mooney

was a butcher's daughter. She was a woman who was quite able to keep things to herself: a determined woman.'[4] These sentences are not as straightforward as they sound. They tell us not necessarily the truth about Mrs Mooney or what God or the world thinks of her, but what she thinks of herself. It is her accent we hear, the precise degree of assertiveness her voice would deliver. But the sentences are still predicated on the assumption that there is a world which language merely negotiates: dappled seaborne clouds would persist even if the English language did not.

Granted. But Joyce was deeply susceptible to the opposite notion, too, that words as such far surpass the character by which they usefully refer to things and help us to administer them. It was Samuel Beckett and not Joyce who wrote: 'Words have been my only loves, not many'. But Joyce might have written it, for the sentiment that finds words purer and richer than anything they merely denote. Some of his styles acknowledge, like Mrs Mooney, a world more or less given; its reality can be manipulated but not, in the end, transformed. But he has other styles which testify not to worlds and realities as given but to another world sustained only by the desire of it. In Joyce's early poems and in the *Portrait,* this world that exists only in the desire of it is represented by poetry, or by phrases of it, remembered and fondled. Sometimes the beauty of the phrase depends upon Stephen's removing it from its context, as if from every mere historical condition, as at one point he removes Luigi Galvani's phrase, 'the enchantment of the heart', and lets it dominate his sentences: 'An enchantment of the heart! The night had been enchanted. In a dream or vision he had known the ecstasy of seraphic life. Was it an instant of enchantment only or long hours and days and years and ages?'

If the world is, according to Wittgenstein, 'everything that is the case', then in reading Joyce we have to assume also a second world, everything that is not the case but is so intensely desired that, so far as the imagination of desire is in question, it amounts to its own case. The two worlds are not, indeed, totally separate; they couldn't be. The first world, even in a life like Joyce's of much grief, is likely to give forth a few consolations, appeasing some old wounds. The second world, so far as it takes a linguistic form, has to admit many echoes from the world it otherwise repudiates. But if there are writers who accept the given world to the extent of annotating it and finding their satisfaction in doing little more, Joyce is not one of them. He is intransigent in desiring a world that never was, or that was only in the poetic fragments that would replace it.

But I have to qualify this report, if only to take account of such a scene as the one in *Ulysses,* the second chapter, where Stephen helps the boy Cyril Sargent with his sums: 'Ugly and futile: lean neck and tangled hair and a stain of ink, a snail's bed. Yet someone had loved him, borne him in her arms and in her heart. But for her the race of the world would have trampled him under foot, a squashed boneless snail.'[5] Richard Blackmur, I recall, once quoted that passage, and distinguished between Stephen Dedalus and Leopold Bloom largely on the strength of it, saying that the passage shows Stephen at his most tender. 'He transcends his intransigence, and comes on the conditions of life – which is where Bloom is all the time.' There again we have the two worlds, and only a different vocabulary for them. Leopold Bloom accepts the conditions of his life and wants only to succeed in forgetting their most painful embodiments – his father's suicide, his son's death, fears for his daughter, and at four o'clock the certainty that Molly is taking Blazes Boylan to her bed. Still, Bloom remains in his conditions and makes the middling best of them. But Stephen resents every condition, and would accept life only if it were another life; except for rare lapses into a more general acknowledgement.

The question is: what form does desire take, in this intransigent sense, when it comes into language and disdains the chore of annotation?

I want to come upon an answer to this a little roundabout. Several years ago the critic Kenneth Burke proposed a certain pattern in the development of a writer. His notion is that most writers start off by writing of themselves and giving every privilege to their own feelings. The ideal form of this phase is the short lyric poem, or the lyrical fiction which is hardly fiction at all. Some writers never escape from this phase. But the major writer escapes at least far enough to acknowledge the existence of other people and to let them live their own lives. Better still if he can imagine other lives, and best of all if these lives are vigorously distinct from his own. If the chronology could be bent a little, we might take Joyce as a case in point. Starting out with early fragile poems, the first version of the *Portrait,* the *Portrait* itself, and the luridly imagined episode that took the form of the play *Exiles.* Then the crucial development in his career would be the diversion of privileged interest from Stephen, the hero of lyrical experience, to Leopold Bloom, who sustains the middling perfection of putting up with things. But *Dubliners* breaks the symmetry of his development, a very early work largely written in 1905 from jottings earlier still. So we have to say that there were at least early stirrings, even in the lyrical or self-expressive phase, of the recognitions that issued fully in *Ulysses.* But the pattern has further to go. It sometimes happens, even in a book which takes communication as its morality, that a writer in the process of imagining lives other than his own will come upon possibilities purely internal to his medium, possibilities which surpass the morality of communication. Some writers may glimpse these possibilities and decide to leave them alone, presumably because they find security in the bond of communication and would not want to be released from it. But there are other writers who, coming upon those possibilities, will insist on exploiting them as if 'to the end of the line'. To those writers, if something is glimpsed as possible, it becomes an aesthetic necessity; it must be done.

You see already how the pattern might be called upon to explain Joyce's development in his later work. In *Ulysses,* for the most part, he accepts the bond of communication. At least in the first half of the book he rarely affronts his readers, or confounds them. But it is clear that as the book proceeded Joyce indeed came upon purely internal possibilities, which offered themselves as a pun might offer itself to someone in a conversation, and in some of the late chapters of the book, tentatively, he explores those possibilities. Several years later he develops them with full panache in *Finnegans Wake,* where he sees a possibility and never looks back.

In *Ulysses* the two worlds I have referred to – we can now call them the world of conditions and the world of desire –

are generously projected. Every reader of the book warms to
its presentation of the sights, sounds, and smells of Dublin,
the noise of its streets, the lore and gossip, both eloquent to
the pitch of exorbitance. If you want an example of reality
which gives the impression that it hadn't to be imagined at all
but only transcribed, think of Paddy Dignam's funeral, and
the man in the macintosh who turns up in Glasnevin. Bloom
wonders who he is: 'Now who is that lankylooking galoot
over there in the macintosh? Now who is he I'd like to know?
Now, I'd give a trifle to know who he is. Always someone
turns up you never dreamt of.' Bloom counts the mourners
at the graveside, and makes the man in the macintosh number
thirteen. The reporter Hynes is listing the mourners, and after
a misunderstanding with Bloom he puts the stranger down
as Mr M'Intosh. And so on. The stranger turns up again,
indeed several times, later in the book; or at least he enters
into Bloom's meanderings. So he can readily stand for the
supreme condition of their being life at all, a life that has to
be lived rather than imagined.

Now the world of desire is so pervasive in *Ulysses* that there
is no point in giving an example of it; it is incorrigible. It is
there in every daydream, every swoon of apprehension, every
poetic phrase which surpasses whatever it denotes. It is there
whenever an event at large is seen and pondered and fondled
in someone's mind to the point at which it is no longer merely
an external event but has become an internal event of still
richer account in that character. The Marxist critic Fredric
Jameson [7] has gone so far as to say that the fundamental device
of *Ulysses* is a technique by which events in an alienated world
are converted into inwardness, where they are reconciled by
the tone in which they are received. Jameson resents the
technique, for obvious reasons. As a Marxist, he wants to
change the world of conditions. He does not want to further
the possibility of leaving the world as it is by having its
conditions end up, accepted for the most part, in Bloom's
meandering mind. If everything that crosses Bloom's path can
be transposed into himself, converted into inwardness, there
is no urgent reason to change the world. It is for this reason
that a Marxist resents the stratagems of consciousness, the
techniques of inwardness by which a reconciling tone displaces

every political incitement.

The particular possibility Joyce came upon in writing the later chapters of *Ulysses* was that of dissolving the barrier between one world and another, a procedure which might correspond to dissolving the distinction between the conscious and the unconscious phases of the mind. Language is not responsive to transitions, states of feeling which melt or merge in one another beyond rational discrimination. The reason is that words in conventional forms are separated from one another, and tend to divide states of feeling into particles which do not correspond to the history of the feeling it denotes. Music was the most fascinating art to writers in the last years of the nineteenth century because it is good at transitions. Think of the 'natural history' of feelings as we hear them in Wagner and Debussy; there are no fractures, no clear demarcation between one feeling and another. The deficiency of words is not the indeterminacy which is said to afflict them but the abrupt demarcation between one word and the next, which corresponds to nothing in anyone's experience.

Suppose you wanted to write a book, a kind of dream-play, in which the conscious and unconscious phases of the mind would be blurred beyond rational redemption, in which the conventional distinctions on which we rely would be dissolved – distinctions between past and present, the dead and the living, one person and another, history and myth, animal and human. When Joyce walked through the British Museum and looked at the Assyrian and Egyptian monuments, he felt, as he told Arthur Power, that 'the Assyrians and Egyptians understood better than we do the mystery of animal life, a mystery which Christianity has almost ignored. Since the advent of Christianity', he said, 'we seem to have lost our sense of proportion, for too great stress is laid on man.'[8] Scholars have argued that it was the Egyptian *Book of the Dead* which most inspired Joyce to write a book in which such conventionally useful distinctions would be dissolved. The *Book* tells of the journey of the dead to achieve eternal justification and resurrection in Amenti, the Elysian fields. The deceased assumed the power of the gods, and above all identified himself with Osiris, the type of death and resurrection. Osiris and his sister-wife each played many roles, their personalities constantly dissolving and forming again, as in a dream of being. The material Joyce read in Sir E. A. Wallis Budge's *Gods of the Egyptians,*[9] and several other similar books, gave him the motif of death and resurrection in a tradition far removed from the Christian one, and therefore free of the historical complication in a doctrine too familiar for his purposes.

Finnegans Wake is still a book in English, of a sort. Or rather, the structure of such divisions as it allows, whether we call them sentences or not, is recognisably English. But the words are confounded by taking to themselves diverse linguistic affiliations and echoes from a dozen languages. Some parts of it are more speakable than others, notably the famous section we can still hear in Joyce's recording of it, the scene in which washerwomen gossip as they do their chores on the banks of the Liffey.

But by and large, the book remains a private place for scholars.

That situation may change. *Ulysses* was many years in the world before anyone but a professional student thought of reading it. Now it is widely read, and not merely studied. The history of Radio Telefís Éireann will document as a notable exploit the reading of the entire book, an act sure to gain entry to the *Guinness Book of Records* not only for its length but for its bravado. *Finnegans Wake,* too, may have such a future, though many of its sequences seem to defeat the speaking voice. But I doubt if the *Wake* will ever be readable unless we extend our notion of language to accommodate its procedures. Instead of receiving words as tokens of reference and vehicles of a meaning separable from the words, we would have to think of words as what the *Wake* once calls them, 'words of silent power', for which the required authority is not the dictionary but the history of magical practice. And if we want a motto from the *Wake* itself, there is one on page 570, a reference to Thoth, the god of speech, magic, and writing, secretary to the gods, and, as Mark Troy has pointed out, responsible for the writing of the *Book of the Dead.*[10] So we read on page 570: '. . . Well but remind to think, you were yestoday Ys Morganas war and that it is always to-morrow in toth's tother's place. Amen.'[11]

I have mentioned 'words of silent power' for a more available reason. A well-known episode in the *Portrait of the Artist* has Stephen engaged in a little struggle of words with the English Dean of Studies in the university, a struggle on the respective provenance of the words 'funnel' and 'tundish'. Stephen wins the occasion, for what it is worth, but then he starts thinking of the English language, and of the Dean's possession of it. He felt, we read: 'with a smart of dejection that the man to whom he was speaking was a countryman of Ben Jonson.' He thought 'the language in which we are speaking is his before it is mine. How different are the words *home, Christ, ale, master,* on his lips and on mine! I cannot speak or write these words without unrest of spirit. His language, so familiar and so foreign, will always be for me an acquired speech. I have not made or accepted its words. My voice holds them at bay. My soul frets in the shadow of his language.'[12]

I have quoted that passage mainly to remark upon the edginess of Joyce's own relation to the English language. It is not precisely the edginess of those Irish writers in our own day who feel that they must retain contact, in some way, with the Irish language, either by writing in it, as several poets do and as Michael Hartnett has given up writing in English to do; or by translating it, as Thomas Kinsella, Seamus Heaney, and other poets have done, into an English mindful of the language it has displaced. I cannot hear in Joyce any such misgiving. I don't recognise any evidence that he ever wanted to write in Irish or to pay his tribute to a dispossessed language and its culture. But I think he needed, as Stephen did, the sentiment of being homeless, at odds with whatever offered itself to him as his condition.

There are some artists who need restlessness as others need peace: as Goldsmith said of someone, 'he only frets to keep himself employed'. Joyce did not say, as Stephen did, 'My soul frets in the shadow of his language', but Joyce, too, cultivated a fretting if not a fretful relation to the English language, and, I think, because he needed the conditions which could only be met by an exertion of will and power. He needed to refuse the 'mother tongue', as Stephen needed to refuse his mother's death-bed request.

Joyce's exercise of will and power is clear in several aspects of his career. He wrote in an English which he thought of as something to be mastered. He did not think of his work in that language as a work of collaboration with the great writers in the English tradition, or with the values that tradition embodied. F. R. Leavis often maintained that William Blake's genius was most fully manifested in his sense of being an English poet, a poet, that is, engaged in 'a continuous creative collaboration' with and within the English language. There is nothing of such a sentiment in Joyce's relation to English. How could there be, given that he was an Irishman whether he liked that fate or not?

But he also exercised his power nearer home and homelessness. If he had been willing to subdue his pride, he could have aligned himself with the aims of the Irish Literary Revival, a movement, after all, hospitable to the extremely diverse purposes reflected in George Moore, Yeats, Douglas Hyde, Lady Gregory and J. M. Synge. But he was never willing to subdue his pride for such a cause. Indeed, while his work is full of Yeatsian echoes and allusions, he took Yeats as his chief antagonist. There is a current theory of literary history, best recommended by the critic Harold Bloom, that a strong writer turns his strength to account by choosing a great precursor, a major writer different in the kind of his genius and incorrigible in its degree; by choosing him and engaging him in a struggle as if to the death. In that sense, Yeats is Joyce's chosen and fated precursor. Joyce had to swerve from Yeats's way of being a genius, and disown its forms to accomplish his own.

So it was almost inevitable that Joyce would choose not any of the Irish ways of being a genius, but the European way. I have never felt much inclined to lose sleep over Joyce's exile, or the conditions which allegedly drove him from Ireland. The truth is that he was not driven, unless we mean that he was driven by a fretting and chafing sense of any conditions offered him. The collusion of chance and choice made Joyce the kind of artist he became; chance, by making him an Irishman and keeping him in that condition; choice, by which I mean his choosing to become an artist of European scope and grandeur, blood-brother to Dante, Shakespeare, Swift,

Flaubert, Pater and Ibsen.

A European, in that sense, is something you choose to become. You cannot be born to it. You are not a European merely by being born in France or Germany. Yeats chose Plato and Plotinus for friends, but the choice was merely opportunistic, not a matter of principle. Joyce's choice of Europe was indeed a matter of principle. I think he wanted to live in such a spirit as to make home whatever he chose to remember, and thereafter to have a chiefly nomadic relation to life. This suggests that he wanted the unsettled conditions from which the artistic detachment which we associate with Flaubert would emerge. But I have been persuaded by William Empson to emphasise rather the example of Ibsen. Empson has argued that Joyce's belief 'that in Ibsen Europe was going ahead with its own large development was what prevented him from being an Irish Nationalist.'[13] There's much to be said for that view, and a good deal of biographical evidence in its favour, starting with Joyce's learning enough Norwegian as a young man to read Ibsen in the original, and publishing a high-flying article in the *Fortnightly Review* in 1900 to praise Ibsen and, I think, to tell the world where his own artistic eyes were turning.

But in any case Joyce gave definitive form, starting with the last pages of the *Portrait,* to the desire which begins in Ireland and defines itself in Europe, seeking not its fortune but its providential form. In his domestic life he spoke more Italian than French, more French than English. *Finnegans Wake* is Irish of necessity, European in its diction, and Egyptian in its major mythology. That should be enough to be going on with, if an art of European scale is in question.

As an Irishman by necessity, Joyce set astir a fiction, as in Flann O'Brien's *At Swim-Two-Birds* and *The Third Policeman,* of comic ingenuity, the words on the page in blatant disproportion to any use they might be turned to. As a European on principle, he set a pattern for the disinterested occupation of space. Its chief exponent since Joyce has been Samuel Beckett, a writer as different from Joyce as he could reasonably be, given so many similarities. But as soon as you start naming names to denote such consequences and consanguinities, there is no end to it.

Meanwhile we proceed. *Finnegans Wake* is clearly the next item, after forty-four years in which most of us have left it well alone. Is it an example of language secreting itself from resources as promiscuous as Europe itself? Or, beneath every surface, is it a story not much different from any other? The most recent suggestion I have seen is Hugh Kenner's, that the book started out from some sense of Erskine Childers' execution in 1922 and became a story about a family in Chapelizod, ending in the dormant mind of the mother, widowed now, the morning after, 'trying not to awaken to awareness that her husband lies beside her no longer'.[14] We could do worse than begin with that end.

8. Literary Autobiography in Twentieth-Century Ireland

Terence Brown

> *'I think we shall live as a generation as the Young
> Irelanders did. We shall not be detached figures.'*
> W. B. YEATS.

In 1913 W. B. Yeats wrote to Katharine Tynan, the poet and
novelist, about her recently published *Twenty-five Years:
Reminiscences* in a letter which alerts us to the role
autobiography could play in a literary movement. 'I have often
felt,' wrote Yeats, 'that the influence of our movement on the
generation immediately following us will very largely depend
on the way in which the personal history is written. It has
always been so in Ireland. Our interest in the Young Irelanders
was largely a personal interest and I doubt if one would have
cared for them half so much but for Gavan Duffy's books.
Even the Dark Rosaleen was only part of the drama explained
to us by Duffy. I am glad, too, that George Moore's
disfiguring glass will not be the only glass. . .'[1]

Yeats in 1913 could not have known in how many differing
glasses the Irish literary movement to which he was committed
would be reflected before it had run its course, not reckoning
on Joyce's satiric reflecting glass in the Scylla and Charybdis
episode in *Ulysses,* nor on the fact that through autobiography
after autobiography the main and lesser personages of the
period would weave their way like characters in a never-
ending fictional saga. Moore, Yeats, Synge, O'Casey, Edward
Martyn, Gogarty, George Russell, Hyde, Lady Gregory,
Maud Gonne, Osborn Bergin, Kuno Meyer, Thomas
MacDonagh *et alia* comprise the *dramatis personae* of a drama
enacted in the memories of a plethora of autobiographers
through which, in part, we gain our sense of the period.

Yeats, in his letter to Katharine Tynan, was, of course,
expressing his irritation at what had already appeared of

George Moore's three-volume autobiographical work *Hail and Farewell* which Moore had begun publishing in 1911. There had been much in *Hail and Farewell* to annoy the poet even by 1913 when two volumes were out. And before the final volume appeared in 1914 Moore published a section of it in the *English Review* in which he suggested that Yeats's friend, admirer and patron, Lady Gregory, had been guilty of proselytism in her early years. That would have been enough to rouse the ardent poet to the defence of a lady and rise he did. But one also suspects that it was Moore's portrait of Yeats himself throughout the work that gave most offence. No man would really care to be described as Moore describes Yeats at the opening of his book, as 'lost in meditation before a white congregation of swans assembled on the lake, looking himself in his old cloak like a huge umbrella left behind by some pic-nic party,'[2] a joke Moore thought so well of that he repeated it later in the work. Nor could Yeats have much cared for the highly satiric portrait Moore was to paint of him in the third volume of the trilogy, *Vale,* where the poet is seen berating the Irish middle classes shortly after a remunerative lecture tour in the United States had left him the owner of an opulent fur coat.

But there were much more substantial reasons why Yeats would have found *Hail and Farewell* a distasteful misrepresentation of his movement. For Moore in his book was offering a massive critique of the Irish literary movement's significance and cultural potential. Not only does Moore insist on treating the whole enterprise in mock-epic fashion, with a comic zest that ultimately proposes Moore himself as an utterly improbable Messiah, a suffering servant of an ungrateful people, but he implies that the very notion of an Irish Renaissance is inappropriate in the circumstances of the Ireland of his day. This latter notion he dismisses by implication when, in what appears a digression, he describes a visit to Wagner's Bayreuth where an ideal of art in relationship with society is presented in the image of a theatre, beside which the exploits of the Irish Literary Theatre must appear hopelessly inadequate if not ridiculous. The idea of Irish Renaissance is subject to further erosion in the evocations of Moore's boyhood in a vigorous County Mayo household and young manhood in an adventurous artistic community in Paris that both suggest an energy and sense of social and imaginative brio in comparison with which the realities of twentieth-century Ireland must seem only residually vital. And conclusively, in Moore's sense of things, the Ireland in which Yeats and Lady Gregory so ambitiously labour is hopelessly subject to the rule of a philistine priesthood that in its authoritarian obscurantism must render all artistic and cultural endeavour futile. Synge is granted a fundamental artistic integrity; at a lesser level Yeats is allowed his genius. But only George Russell really escapes Moore's pervasive sense of the ridiculous, achieving a kind of sainthood in the author's portrayal of him as a blend of unselfconsciously practical activist and holy fool.

It would be quite wrong to read Yeats's autobiographical prose works (ultimately published as *Autobiographies*) as simply the poet's effort to set the record straight. They are much more than a reply to *Hail and Farewell,* primarily being a broodingly powerful record of the recreative powers of the self in relation to its own past. But in important senses they are a riposte to the trilogy, perhaps, the least of them being that they allow Yeats to have his say on Moore himself.

In *Dramatis Personae* he is damned as 'more mob than man'[3] and the poet has him in the same work sitting 'among art students, young writers about to become famous, in some café; a man carved out of a turnip looking out of astonished eyes.'[4]

Yeats's first autobiographical prose work was published in 1916 as *Reveries over Childhood and Youth*. He had begun work on this in 1914 and when it was complete he wrote a further autobiographical draft which was to serve as a basis for part of the autobiographies he was to publish as *Four Years* (1922), *The Trembling of the Veil* (1922) and *Dramatis Personae* (1935). These, along with *Reveries over Childhood and Youth,* constitute the greater part of the volume *Autobiographies* which was published posthumously in 1955.[5] This final work, a compilation of most of Yeats's various autobiographical essays, affords an interpretation of the literary movement in striking contrast to that which Moore had supplied in *Hail and Farewell*.

Where Moore's curiously meandering progress, in which
much crucial material had appeared as extensive digressions,
suggested a blending of past and present, in Yeats's work the
past remains the past. Accordingly, where Moore's work
seems to imply that the Mayo boyhood he enjoyed somehow
had greater significance than the more modern events he
records, and could not be equalled in the contemporary world,
Yeats treats his Sligo background as something which in no
way transcends subsequent experience. A key sentence in
Reveries over Childhood and Youth is therefore: 'I remember
little of childhood but its pain. I have grown happier with
every year of life as though conquering something in myself,
for certainly my miseries were not made by others but were
part of my own mind.'[6] Furthermore, Moore had suggested
that nineteenth-century art, the music and theatre of Wagner,
the painting of Manet, were normative for twentieth-century
Ireland ('It took fifteen years for the light of Manet's genius
to reach Ireland,' he remarked contemptuously.)[7] Yeats has
none of this. In *The Tragic Generation* he presents himself as
the charmed survivor of a nineteenth-century decadence that
destroyed a generation, leaving him to help fashion a fresh
artistic future in a new century and a new country, in the face
of almost universal pessimism. 'Why,' he asks in *The Tragic
Generation* as late as the 1920s, 'why are these strange souls
born everywhere today, with hearts that Christianity, as
shaped by history, cannot satisfy? Our love-letters wear out
our love; no school of painting outlasts its founders, every
stroke of the brush exhausts the impulse, pre-Raphaelitism
had some twenty years: Impressionism thirty perhaps.'[8] The
modern artist must make it new; so it does not surprise that
the section following in *The Trembling of the Veil* is entitled
The Stirring of the Bones in which the poet declares his faith
that the Literary Revival, particularly in the noble work of
Synge and in that of Lady Gregory has done much to 'deepen
Irish imagination'[9] in a way that Moore with his obsession
with Catholicism's baneful influence could not comprehend.
'I have written,' he declares, 'these words instead of leaving
all to posterity. . . that young men, to whom recent events
are often more obscure than those long past, may learn what
debts they owe and to what creditor.'[10]

Whatever the young were to feel about their debts and creditors, they were to emulate their elders in the production of autobiography. Seán O'Casey, fifteen years Yeats's junior, was to produce his own autobiographical prose works in six volumes between 1939 and 1954; Frank O'Connor (born 1903) published his *Only Child* in 1959 and his *My Father's Son* appeared posthumously in 1968; Sean O'Faolain (born 1900) published his *Vive Moi* in 1965; Austin Clarke (born 1896) his *Twice Round the Black Church* in 1962 and his *A Penny in the Clouds* in 1968. And they were all in their various ways to afford Yeats and his contemporaries the recognition that apportioning them parts in their own works implied. Our view of the Literary Revival is conditioned therefore not only by the records of the prime movers but by those of its inheritors.

O'Casey, of the writers mentioned above, had been closest to the centres of energy about which the idea of a Literary Revival had gathered. For it had been his three major plays, *The Shadow of a Gunman, Juno and the Paycock* and *The Plough and the Stars*, which had revived the fortunes of the Abbey Theatre in the 1920s and had brought it once more to the forefront of the Irish public's attention. But he was never to join the upper circle of those who felt the movement was their own. And his treatment by Yeats when he submitted his play *The Silver Tassie* to the Abbey for production could scarcely have allowed him to feel that he had been accorded full membership of the movement. It may be possible therefore to read parts of his *Autobiographies* as polemical expositions of how different he was from the other writers of the period, in origin and social experience. This one certainly senses in the first volume where his sufferings and those of his mother in the midst of Dublin's destitution are emphasised to the point of this reader's credulity. But there is no mistaking the author's sense of outrage at the pain, misery and degradation that he believes had been his lot in Ireland's capital. And more generally O'Casey's huge work, flawed as it is by linguistic bombast and by lack of verbal control, creates a powerful impression of a modern Ireland struggling to be born. The hero Johnny/Seán Casside is caught up in the cataclysmic events that drag a Victorian society, ruled by God, Queen

Victoria, Church and State, struggling into a twentieth century of revolutionary hope and disillusionment. In all of this the Literary Revival and the major figures associated with it are not allowed a dominant role in a period which saw the fall of Parnell, saw Jim Larkin and James Connolly bestride the stage of Irish history, the foundation of the Gaelic League, the Irish Volunteers, the Irish Citizen Army, the violence of the Rising, the War of Independence and Civil War. But in the matter of *The Silver Tassie* O'Casey acknowledged that Yeats too was a Titan. 'He read the letters again: the one from Yeats was the one to be answered. Seán could not but believe that the play's rejection had been decided upon before the play had been sent. To answer Yeats would be a dangerous thing to do. Yeats in his greatness had influence everywhere, and the world of literature bowed down before him. But answered he must be, and answered be would be, even though the strife meant the end of Seán.'[11].

Austin Clarke had reason to resent Yeats's treatment of him too. For Yeats had chosen not to include any poems by Clarke in the *Oxford Book of Modern Verse* (published in 1936) of which he was editor, while including many verses by poets Clarke must have considered his artistic inferiors. In the second volume of Clarke's autobiography *A Penny in the Clouds* Yeats is sensed from the first pages as an intimidatory presence admired by the younger poet as a master poetic craftsman and theatrical innovator; but he is also viewed with a wary circumspection and not entirely convincing scepticism. Clarke's appreciation of the inheritance of the Literary Revival, however, is related to his gratitude, implicit throughout *A Penny in the Clouds,* that a generation of scholars and poets (of whom Yeats was in the end only one) had made the suppressed, richly humanistic Gaelic civilisation of Ireland available once more to the educated Irish mind. So, much of Clarke's second autobiographical volume suggests how liberating a force the Gaelic tradition could be in helping to heal a psyche that had been profoundly disturbed by the dark puritanical Catholicism which he had explored with an almost Joycean precison in his first volume of autobiography *Twice Round the Black Church.* There, only the consciousness of the mysterious givenness of the material world, especially in a feeling for water as a kind of secular blessing, had saved a sensibility distracted by the anguish of religious guilt, from total disintegraton. In *A Penny in the Clouds* the Gaelic tradition sanctions the first volume's grasp on a sane materialism and helps the poet to break through to personal artistic and sexual freedom, teaching him to trust Nature as a beneficent goddess, whose gifts can sustain the self.

Psychological survival is very much an aspect of Frank O'Connor's two autobiographical volumes. Their account of how the writer emerged from a devastatingly disturbed home in Cork, a home afflicted by the twin evils of alcoholism and poverty, to become one of Ireland's foremost literary figures makes for harrowing, compulsive reading. Devoted to his mother and exhibiting all the signs of a personality marked by oedipal feelings, it was all too likely that O'Connor would seek father-surrogates as he made his turbulent way from adolescence to manhood in the midst of war and civil war. There were those ready to play the role – Daniel Corkery, the writer's first mentor, then George Russell and eventually Yeats himself who gave O'Connor the support, advice and respect he felt able to offer to scarcely no other of O'Connor's generation. The result is that Yeats in *My Father's Son* is offered a kind of veneration that survives the plotting and counter-plotting, the failures and disappointments of the later years of the poet's involvement with the board of the Abbey Theatre. Yeats appears here as a portrait of the imaginative man in old age, still driven by his passions and angers, fighting heroically to the last, essentially redeemed from the daily spite of an unmannerly town by an indestructible magnanimity. O'Connor's is probably the most romantic account we have of Yeats's later life and of his contribution over a life-time to Irish letters. Indeed, O'Connor's entire autobiography might be described as a study in the romance of literature. For life is seen throughout in terms of the kind of literature O'Connor himself most admired, the kind which values personality and its dramatic expression in a distinctive voice in the way, in fact, his own short stories do.

Romantic individualism governs O'Connor's assessment of the political and military events of 1916-23 in which he played a part. In that period Ireland is imagined as having acted almost in terms of a personality that for a brief, all-too-brief moment, had achieved a condition of total integration and could accordingly express itself without ambiguity or self-consciousness. O'Connor's word for this is 'improvisation' which suggests both theatricality and insecure spontaneity. Ireland, he asserted of the revolution and its disillusioned aftermath, had 'improvised a government, and clearly no government that claimed even a fraction less than the imaginary government had claimed could attract the loyalty of young men and women with imagination. They were like a theatre audience that having learned to dispense with fortuitous properties, lighting, and scenery and begun to appreciate theatre in the raw, were being asked to content themselves with cardboard and canvas. Where there is nothing, there is reality.'[12]

Sean O'Faolain's *Vive Moi* is much preoccupied with coming to terms personally with the same events. The relationship of literature to reality also engages his fundamental attention. For most of the book, however, the Literary Revival as an individual literary phenomenon is not a major concern. It is rather the phenomenon of literature itself that absorbs him. But his analysis of the period is, significantly, couched at a crucial stage in Yeatsian terminology. Ireland had been from 1916 to 1922, O'Faolain's argument runs, in the grip of a powerful mesmerising dream, but tragically had lacked a coherent, realisable political programme. The revolutionaries had been idealists in thrall like himself before 'the golden ikons of the past'.[13] In the end he has to admit, drawing on the language of Yeats's poem 'Blood and the Moon': 'We were all idealists, self-crazed by abstractions, lost in the labyrinths of the dreams to which we had retreated from this pragmatical pig of a world.'[14] That world (and the final metaphor is Yeats's) O'Faolain clearly felt should be the politician's and the artist's proper domain; for O'Faolain himself it must be the drab, provincial reality of modern Ireland which he must explore in literature. Idealism both political and literary would like to pretend it did not exist or could be ignored. O'Faolain the artist knew he must write of it. When at the end of his socially and culturally analytic autobiography he attempts his own estimate of Yeats's example as an artist and his significance for Irish letters, it is in a general context of idealism sensed as in decline. Yeats is conceived as part of that period of high idealism which now must give way to a period when artists should have a firmer grasp on fact: He writes of four dinners at which the members of Yeats's Irish Academy of Letters met in the 1930s because, he suggests, 'they may re-evoke the sense that I gradually got of a tide receding about me.'[15] And although he affords Yeats the high compliment of stating 'he had been our inspiration and our justification in the sense that all the rest of us younger men and women could not, between us, represent literature with anything like his achievement and authority in the eyes of the public'[16] he must also enter a crucial criticism: 'It was his need of nature, as poet and man, to live a foot off the ground, a foot or two or more, away from common life.'[17] As artist he had committed the error that O'Faolain's generation had committed as political activists. *Vive Moi* in its detached sober description and appraisal of that common life – in pre-revolutionary Cork, in post–civil-war Ennis, County Clare, and in Dublin – implies a different literary relationship with the ordinary than Yeats ever contemplated. The work as a whole proposes a reinterpretation of the Ireland Yeats had dreamed 'terrible and gay' ('The Municipal Gallery Re-visited'), and appropriately ends with a critical if respectful analysis of the poet.

O'Faolain is probably the most deliberately analytic in historical terms of the Irish literary autobiographers of this century. There have been others who have lacked any so palpable design whether upon the Literary Revival, the Nationalist movement or anything else. Indeed, almost at an opposite pole to O'Faolain's historical/cultural theorising one might cite Liam O'Flaherty's *Shame the Devil* (1934), an uninhibitedly self-absorbed study of psychological disturbance and recovery related with the frenetic pace of a sensationalist fiction. Or one might cite Patrick Kavanagh's slightly *faux-naïve* account in *The Green Fool* (1938) of childhood, youth and young-manhood in a County Monaghan almost hermetically sealed by its own sense of the local, from any more general experience of things. And that is not to mention Terence de Vere White's wittily urbane and occasionally hilarious account in *A Fretful Midge* (1957) of a middle-class Dublin Catholic childhood and a manhood troubled in social and cultural senses only by the twin mysteries of the painter Jack Yeats's lack of genuine international reputation in his lifetime and Eamon de Valera's very great political success. Nor, indeed, is it to dwell on Louis MacNeice's almost Proustian recall of the delights and horrors of a Northern Irish childhood in an Anglican rectory and of the sense of release offered by the Oxford of the 1920s in *The Strings are False* (published posthumously in 1965). And Hugh Leonard's *Home Before Night* (1979), that painfully comic study of the anguish of adolescence, can only be seen as proffering a view of Ireland, with or without literary and political movements, in its prevailingly sardonic attitude to almost everybody and everything. As Brendan Behan's masterpiece *Borstal Boy* (1958) proves, were proof necessary, a raw personal history vibrantly realised can have its own compelling interest, irrespective of the literary or historical movements that have so often added significance to autobiographical endeavour in Ireland in the twentieth century.

9. Prose Writing Translated from the Irish

Proinsias Ó Conluain

According to Dr Douglas Hyde, the first English translation from an Irish prose work was Conall Mageoghegan's rendering of *The Annals of Clonmacnoise*, made in 1627 but not published until 1896. Poetry had been translated earlier, mainly, it seems, so that the English overlords might have some insight into the minds of those people called Bards who, as they saw it, glorified not the civilising Englishman but 'whomsoever they finde to be most licentious of life, most bold and lawlesse in his doings, most dangerous and desperate in all parts of disobedience and rebellious disposition.'[1]

Edmund Spenser was appointed secretary to the Lord Lieutenant for Ireland in 1580. In 1586 Queen Elizabeth I granted him over three thousand acres in County Cork out of the forfeited lands of the Earl of Desmond. It was there, in the castle of Kilcolman, surrounded by the 'bandit country' of the time, that he wrote his best-known poem, *The Fairie Queene*. As an English administrator he was interested in the outpourings of the Irish bards as potentially subversive – as 'tending for the most part to the hurt of the English' – but as a poet and translator of poets he was inquisitive about their quality as poetry. 'Have they any art in their compositions?' he asked, 'or bee they anything wittie or well savoured, as poemes should be?' He answered his own question: 'Yea, truely, I have caused divers of them to be translated unto me, that I might understand them, and surely they savoured of sweet wit and good invention, but skilled not of the goodly ornaments of poetry; yet were they sprinkled with some pretty flowers of their natural device, which gave good grace and comlinesse unto them, the which it is great pity to see abused, to the gracing of wickednes and vice, which with good usage would serve to adorne and beautifie vertue. This evil custome therefore needeth reformation.'[2]

What poems in Irish Spenser saw as 'gracing wickedness
and vice' it is impossible now to say, because the translations,
whether in prose or verse, have not survived and his references
are much too imprecise. We have to move on towards the end
of the eighteenth century before we find any serious effort at
translating into English. Joseph C. Walker's *Historical Memoirs
of the Irish Bards,* published in 1786, contained a number of
poems by Carolan, along with verse translations, and in the
years which followed, it was often an interest in the native
music and song, in the tunes to which songs were sung, that
led to the original works in Irish and a desire to have them
translated.

Bunting's first *Collection of the Ancient Irish Music,* published
in 1796 or 1797, had no originals – titles only – and no
translations. That was despite the fact that he had at his disposal
literal prose translations of most of the songs which had been
written down in Irish by his helpers, Patrick Lynch and James
Cody. When he did get around to providing English versions
in his second volume (1809) he elected to publish verse
translations by Thomas Campbell and others which were light
years removed from the sense and spirit of the originals.

Of the early translators, the most influential was undoubtedly Charlotte Brooke whose *Reliques of Irish Poetry* was
published in 1789 and included poems from the Red Branch
and Fenian cycles, with translations – a useful corrective to
Macpherson's *Ossian* which she had read some time after its
first publication nearly thirty years earlier. Macpherson's
work, even if only remotely related to 'Ancient poetry. . .
translated from the Gaelic or Erse language', as he claimed,
could still be seen as 'the first manifestation of the Gaelic genius
in the English tongue'.[3]

Charlotte Brooke brought interest in the old literature a
step further, not so much by the quality of her translations,
which indeed were long-winded, uninspired and highly
artificial, as by indicating the sources on which those who
followed her might draw. Unlike Macpherson, she gave some
of the Gaelic originals and for the first time brought the
Cuchulainn and Fionn Mac Cumhaill and Oisin, so distorted
by Macpherson, to the attention of the English-speaking

world. The Romantic movement in European literature, with its leanings towards strange or vanishing cultures, the Ossianic and similar societies, the Celtic Twilight and the Gaelic League, all in their different ways helped the process of enlightenment. By the beginning of this century the Irish, the German and other continental scholars had been to work on the sagas and hero-tales and a good deal of the old literature was being published. However, as the number of people who could read or write Irish was still very limited, the question of translation was always to the fore. In the same year as the Gaelic League was founded (1893), Stopford Brooke was writing 'on the Need and Use of getting Irish Literature into the English Tongue': 'When we have got the old Irish legendary tales rendered into fine prose and verse,' he said, 'I believe we shall open out English poetry to a new and exciting world, an immense range of subjects, entirely fresh and full of inspiration. . . then we may bring England and Ireland into a union which never can suffer separation and send another imaginative force on earth which may (like Arthur's tale) create Poetry for another thousand years.'[4]

Stopford Brooke's idea of cementing a union of England and Ireland through a new literature based on translation from the Irish was not exactly what the founders of the Gaelic League had in mind and it would indeed have been ironic if, for example, *The Love Songs of Connacht,* published in the year of its foundation, or the first volume of the Irish Texts Society, edited by the League's President and published only six years later, should have contributed in any way towards that objective. That Irish Texts Society volume contained two longish stories: Giolla an Fhiugha or *The Lad of the Ferule* and *Eachtra Cloinne righ na hIoruaidhe* or Adventures of the Children of the King of Norway, edited with translation, notes and glossary by Douglas Hyde. It was to be the beginning of a long series of scholarly works which continues to the present day, all with text and translation and the whole *apparatus criticus*. The translations generally are fairly literal, intended primarily for the use of scholars, though some, like Fr Dinneen's translation of Keating's *Foras Feasa ar Éirinn* or Mícheál Mac Craith's version of *Humphrey O'Sullivan's Diary* or *The Life of Hugh Roe O'Donnell* in the English of Fr Denis

Murphy, with emendations by Fr Paul Walsh and Colm Ó
Lochlainn, can be read as interesting prose works in their own
right. A new and more accurate translation of a somewhat
shorter *O'Sullivan's Diary* was prepared some years ago (1979)
by Tomás de Bhaldraithe for the Mercier Press.

The work of Douglas Hyde and the other scholars in the
matter of translation would be hard to over-estimate. Before
the turn of the century Hyde had published, as well as the
books already mentioned, *Beside the Fire,* a collection of Irish
Gaelic folk stories, *The Three Sorrows of Story-telling,* and two
collections from *An Scéalaí Gaelach,* all translated by himself.
In a long preface to *Beside the Fire* he gives a valuable account
of his approach to the business of translation and of how he
arrived at his own particular style. Early in the new century
four of his plays were to be translated by Lady Gregory;
Abhráin atá leagtha ar an Reachtúire or *Songs ascribed to Raftery*
came in Irish and English in 1903 and *The Religious Songs of
Connacht,* a collection of poems, stories, prayers, satires,
ranns, charms, etc., in two volumes in 1905-1906. In the song
collections Hyde gave either verse or prose translations,
sometimes both, and in the preface to *Love Songs of Connacht*
he expressed the hope that the literal translation would be of
some advantage 'to that at present increasing class of Irish men
who take a just pride in their native language and to those
foreigners who, great philologists and etymologists as they
are, find themselves hampered in their pursuit through their
unavoidable ignorance of the modern Irish idiom.'[5]

He was right. The translations were welcomed at home and
abroad. Yeats praised them highly on their first appearance
and modified his praise only slightly in a preface to the limited
edition of the Love Songs, in translation only, published by
the Dun Emer Press in 1904: 'There have been other
translators,' he said, 'but they had a formal eighteenth-century
style that took what Dr Hyde would call "the sap and pleasure"
out of simple thought and emotion. Their horses were always
steeds and their cows kine. . . Dr Hyde's prose translations. . . are I think even better than his verse ones; but even
he cannot always escape from the influence of his predecessors
when he rhymes in English. His imagination is indeed at its
best only when he writes in Irish, or in that beautiful English

of the country people who remember too much Irish to talk like a newspaper, and I commend his prose comments to all who can delight in fine prose.'[6]

Hyde's prose translations 'in that beautiful English of the country people' had an important influence on all who were later to write in some form of the dialect of English spoken in Ireland – on Lady Gregory and Pádraic Colum, for example, and in particular on John M. Synge. 'The Love Songs of Connacht,' says Ernest Boyd, 'were the constant study of the author of The Playboy, whose plays testify, more than those of any other writer, to the influence of Hyde's prose.'[7] The constant juxtaposition of Irish and English then common had, in Boyd's opinion, profoundly affected the form of modern Anglo-Irish literature: 'Instead of the haphazard, and usually quite false, idioms and accent which at one time were the convention in all reproductions of English as spoken in Ireland, the Literary Revival has given us the true form of Anglo-Irish, so that our literature represents perfectly the old Gaelic spirit in its modern garb.'[8]

But Hyde's influence was to be reflected in different ways. Lady Gregory, following his example, produced her Cuchulain of Muirthemne in 1902 – the Story of the Men of the Red Branch of Ulster, arranged and put into English, as the sub-title had it – and her Gods and Fighting Men, a companion volume, two years later: the story of the Tuatha De Danann and of the Fianna of Ireland. Both books had a preface by Yeats, and both he praised highly, the first as 'the best book that has ever come out of Ireland', because, as he said, 'the stories which it tells are the chief part of Ireland's gift to the imagination of the world – and it tells them perfectly for the first time.'[9]

Yeats, though he had no Irish himself, appreciated the difficulties of translators and in writing his preface he was probably thinking of the numerous scholars who had already given us versions of the Irish hero-tales but whose concern was more with linguistics than literature:

Translators from the Irish have hitherto retold one story or the other from some one version, and not often with any fine understanding of English, of those changes of rhythm for instance that are changes of the sense. They have translated the best and fullest manuscripts they knew,

as accurately as they could, and that is all we have the right
to expect from the first translators of a difficult and old
literature. But few of the stories really begin to exist as
great works of imagination until somebody has taken the
best bits out of many manuscripts. . . Lady Gegory has
done her work of compression and selection at once so
firmly and so reverently that I cannot believe that
anybody, except now and then for a scientific purpose,
will need another text than this. . .[10]

Yeats's greatest praise for Lady Gregory's rendering of the
old stories was that she had discovered a fitting dialect to tell
them in. The dialect, of course, was 'Kiltartanese' – so-called
from Lady Gregory's claim that it was the speech of her
neighbours in Kiltartan to whom she dedicated *Cuchulain*. But
not everyone was as enthusiastic about it as Yeats was. Edward
Martyn, for example, said that nobody in Ireland ever spoke
like that and he parodied the dialect in one of his plays (*The
Dream Physician*) in which he also mocked the 'Celtic glamour'
of Yeats and the antics of 'our funny old Mayo journalist',
George Moore.[11]

   Moore had a curious association with the language revival
movement and with the literary commerce between the two
languages. Around 1901 he decided he had 'a messianic
mission' to return to Ireland and among other things to revive
the Irish language, possibly by writing a masterpiece which
would be translated and first published in that tongue. (To
learn the language himself would be much too difficult; he
would get his nephew to learn it instead.) At one stage he had
collaborated with Yeats in a dramatic version of *Diarmuid and
Grania* from the Ossianic cycle and he had suggested that he
would write his part of the play in French, that Lady Gregory
would translate it into English, that it then be turned into Irish
and then back again into English by Lady Gregory. Needless
to say, nothing came of that particular project but later, on
the suggestion of John Eglinton that he write a story of Irish
life after the manner of Turgenev which would be translated
as a model for prose writers in Irish, he produced an excellent
short story, *The Wedding Gown*. It was published in the *New
Ireland Review,* edited by the Jesuit, Fr Tom Finlay, along with
a translation in Irish by Torna (Tadhg Ó Donncha) under the

ungrammatical title *An Gúna-Phósta*. Other stories followed,
with their parallel Irish versions, until sex and religion raised
their ugly heads and Fr Finlay could no longer accept editorial
responsibility. However, a collection of thirteeen stories in
English, *The Untilled Field,* was published in 1903 – 'the most
perfect book of short stories in contemporary Irish literature',
according to Ernest Boyd. Six of the stories had been published
the previous year in their Irish versions under the title *An
tÚr-Ghort, Sgéaltha le Seórsa Ó Mórdha, aistrighthe ó'n
Sacsbhéarla ag Pádraig Ó Súilleabháin, B.A.* Torna's translation
of *The Wedding Gown* was among the six. Moore had in fact
asked T. W. Rolleston, author, poet and scholar, to translate
that story and some others back into English and he found
them, he said, 'much improved after their bath in Irish.'[12] He
used them for reference in preparing the final English versions
for publication.

Moore's experiment in translation was to have much more
effect on the development of the realistic short story in English
than in setting example for writers in Irish, but Pádraic Pearse,
who was so severely criticised by the traditionalists for his
'explosive openings', could well have been influenced by a
first line like 'Bhí Máire Ní Chrónáin 'na haon iní n agus bhí
a dóithin airgid aici.' Writing in a language in which literary
forms like the novel and short story had no tradition, Pearse
and Pádraic Ó Conaire broke the mould, and signs on it, they
were the most translated authors of the Irish revival up to 1930.

Pearse was himself, of course, a highly competent
translator, particularly of his own work, which was mostly
in Irish in the first instance. His short stories, however,
published in the Collected Works, were translated by Joseph
Campbell after the fashion set by Hyde and they were also
translated by Rev. T. A. Fitzgerald, O.F.M. – four of them
under the title *Connemara Stories* (from *Íosagán agus Scéalta Eile*)
being published in Sydney in 1921. A more recent edition of
the stories in a dual language-book was prepared by Des
Maguire for the Mercier Press in 1968.

Pádraic Ó Conaire probably came under the influence of
Turgenev, or Dostoievsky or whoever, quite independently
of any prompting from George Moore. According to Stephen
MacKenna, his was 'absolutely the only writing you could

imagine a European reading'.[13] He wrote in the modern style but his thoughts seemed to run as much in English as in Irish and this made him an easy author to translate, at least literally. His adventure story for young people, *Tír na nIongantas,* was published by the Powell Press in 1919 and its English equivalent, *The Land of Wonders,* translated by Éamonn Ó Néill, by the Educational Company of Ireland in the same year. Two years later the Talbot Press published *The Woman at the Window and Other Stories,* also translated by Éamonn Ó Néill, the title story being in fact a translation of *Neill* and not of *An Bhean Bhí ag an bhFuinneoig,* another of Ó Conaire's stories.

In 1929, just a year after Pádraic's death, a dozen of his stories were published by the Talbot Press under the title *Field and Fair, Travels with a Donkey in Ireland,* translated by Cormac Breathnach. As that title implies, the stories or essays are from *An Crann Géagach,* one of the most popular of Ó Conaire's works, and they all keep close to the originals in their transfer to English. Ó Conaire continues to be translated and in the most recent collection (1982) fifteen of his stories have been chosen by fifteen translators, the great majority of whom are well known as writers in either Irish or English, or both.

There is a connection between *Field and Fair* and another translator, the man whose drawings illustrated that particular volume, Mícheál Mac Liammóir. Mícheál was as versatile with language and languages as he was as artist or actor. He translated himself, copiously, and no one did it better. As long ago as 1922 he had produced *Oidhcheanna Sidhe,* four stories for young people, with the parallel translation, *Fairy Nights,* and beautiful illustrations by himself. Thirty years later his diary and other essays entitled *Ceo Meala Lá Seaca* were published by Sáirséal agus Dill, and in 1956 *Aisteoirí faoi Dhá Sholas, Dialann Mheánmhara,* came from the same publishers. The second diary, dealing with the Egyptian tour of the Gate Theatre Company, and the diary portion of the earlier book, covering a tour of Germany in 1950, made their way into a book entitled *Each Actor on His Ass,* published in 1961. It was the most unlikely book to have been translated from the Irish language, Mac Liammóir said, 'for not a turf-stack or a wake or even a parish priest appears in sight.'[14] Indeed there could be some argument about how much it is a translation, because Mac Liammóir being Mac Liammóir is not bound by anything he said in Irish in the first place, and being his own translator, is free to add, or excise, or interpret as he sees fit.

Other writers competent in the two languages have put their facility to use. Liam O'Flaherty, for example, wrote some of his best stories in *Dúil,* also published by Sáirséal agus Dill, and some of them have later appeared in English versions, perhaps even without reference to their previous existence. In recent years Liam's nephew, Breandán Ó hEithir, has written one of the best-selling novels in Irish, *Lig Sinn i gCathú,* and an equally popular translation, *Lead Us into Temptation,* which lacks, however, the raciness and often ironic bite of the original.

Máirtín Ó Cadhain, because of his own rich and sometimes esoteric vocabulary, must be one of the most difficult of Gaelic authors to translate but Eoghan Ó Tuairisc overcame most of the difficulties in rendering nine short stories from Ó Cadhain's earlier (and easier) books into English in *The Road to Brightcity.* 'I have tried,' he said, 'to avoid Anglo-Irish dialects and pseudo-dialects; Ó Cadhain's language is cool and classic, and free of the self-conscious mannerisms and the melancholy word-music of the Synge-song school.'[15]

Risteard de Paor, like Ó Tuairisc, wrote well in both languages. Of two novels he wrote in English, one, *The Land of Youth,* was set mainly on an imaginary Aran island. His imaginative account of life on a real Aran island in Irish, *Úll i mBarr an Ghéagáin,* was published in 1959 and a very good translation of it, *Apple on the Treetop,* has been done in recent years by his brother, Victor Power, also a well-known author and dramatist.

It is probably more than coincidence that so many of our translations from Irish have to do with island life or with an individual or community struggling against adversity. Tomás Ó Criomhthain's *An tOileánach* set a pattern not only for autobiography but for a spate of translations into English which had not been seen since the discovery of the ancient sagas. Robin Flower's *Islandman,* however, does not seem to have been in any way definitive in setting a style for translators. Flower did not like the 'literary dialect' sometimes used for translation which, as he said, in books or on the stage had met with considerable success. He thought there was something slightly artificial about it, and often a suggestion of the pseudo-poetic. He opted for 'a plain, straightforward style, aiming at the language of ordinary men who narrate the common experiences of their life frankly and without any cultivated mannerism.'[16]

For their translation of Muiris Ó Súileabháin's *Fiche Bliain ag Fás* Moya Llewelyn Davies and George Thomson chose what they called 'the Irish dialect of English', following the example of Synge, who, they said, 'of all writers in English had the deepest understanding of the Irish-speaking peasantry.'[17] That judgment might be questioned but, fortunately, the translators did not follow the melancholy 'Synge-song' in its worst excesses. In fact their prose is probably much more acceptable to Irish readers than the kind of Hiberno-English which Séamus Ennis chose for his almost word-for-word translation of *Machnamh Sean-Mhná* by Peig Sayers. This was the first of Peig's books to be translated – in 1962, under the title *An Old Woman's Reflections* – and it was a late-comer among the Blasket books in English. Her autobiography, *Peig,* had to wait even longer for a translator but in 1973 it found a good one in Bryan MacMahon. In setting out 'to convey the tone and spirit of the original' MacMahon tried, as he says himself, 'to imagine how Peig Sayers would have told her story, had she been born on a small holding. . . say twenty-five miles to the east of Dunquin, where she and her people, though English-speaking, would have been only one generation removed from Irish as a vernacular.'[18]

The result is a good example of 'the English of Kerry' being used instead of 'the English of Ireland' and it is matched by what we might call 'the English of West Cork' in Riobárd P. Breatnach's *The Man from Cape Clear* from Conchúr Ó Síocháin's *Seanchas Chléire*. The most recent translation in the Blasket Island cycle has Tim Enright following in the footsteps of the master from Listowel, his former teacher. He has translated Mícheál Ó Gaoithín's *Is Trua Ná Fannan an Óige* (Oifig an tSoláthair, 1953), the autobiography of Peig Sayers' son, the poet, who already had the literary experience of

THE GENIUS OF IRISH PROSE

writing down his mother's story for publication. However, the Kerry English may not be to everyone's taste – it's how it might put no glow at all in your ear to be listening to it – or reading it! But then you might enjoy the take-off of the whole lot of them in the Corcadoragha English of *The Poor Mouth,* Patrick C. Power's version of the famous parody, *An Béal Bocht,* by Myles na Gopaleen.

If there is a Blasket cycle of books and translations, there may also be a Routledge and Kegan Paul cycle – also autobiographical. In 1962 the London publishing firm issued two translations, one from the Scots Gaelic and one from the Irish. *The Furrow behind Me* was the story of Angus MacLellan, a Hebridean crofter from South Uist who recorded his recollections in Gaelic for John Lorne Campbell. *The Hard Road to Klondike* was a kind of companion volume, the English version of *Rotha Mór an tSaoil,* the life and adventures of Michael MacGowan as told to folklore collector Seán Ó hEochaidh. The translator was the well-known poet, Valentin Iremonger, proficient and sympathetic but missing many of the nuances of the Donegal Irish. He seemed to be more at ease with Dónall Mac Amhlaigh's *Dialann Deoraí,* translated as *An Irish Navvy* for the same publishers. The original was well laced with the colourful brand of Irish, mixed with words and phrases of English, spoken by the Connemara workers on the building sites of Britain. The conversational character of the writing, described by one critic as 'completely uninhibited by prose style or the O.E.D.',[19] came across in the translation.

That was twenty years ago. Publishers on the trail of translatable books today seem to be looking more towards novels, short stories and works of imagination than to the autobiographies and the 'social documents' which were so popular up to the sixties. It still has to be remembered, however, that even the finest translation is unlikely to be more than a second best, a Flemish tapestry, as someone has said, with the wrong side out.

10. Fable and Fantasy

Augustine Martin

Since the rise of the novel in the eighteenth century, fiction has been predominantly a realistic, social, art form, reflecting accurately, and often minutely, the conditions of life within a recognisable society. Its great practitioners, Jane Austen, Dickens and George Eliot in England, Balzac and Zola in France, rejoiced at the fidelity with which they rendered in imaginative prose the reflection of an actual world – its houses, streets, farm-yards, factories, its mansions and its hovels, its private and public way of life. Fable and fantasy, the less realistic forms of prose fiction, have played very little part in the English tradition – though writers like Lewis Carroll, Kenneth Grahame, G. K. Chesterton, and more recently C. S. Lewis and J. R. R. Tolkien have held a place of special affection among British readers. The Irish nineteenth century tended to follow or parallel the English, with Edgeworth, the Banims, Carleton and George Moore adhering by and large to the realist form and idiom.

There was, however, a dimension of the strange, the magical, the miraculous, always at the margins of these Irish novels: a belief in a world of fairies, witches and ancient gods, a belief in the spiritual and the visionary, a sense of eternity surrounding and sometimes invading the world of time. As the Irish Literary Renaissance grew to a head towards the end of the last century this concern with the unseen world gave rise to a great body of writing – poetry, drama and fiction – which employed the methods of fable and fantasy to express its peculiar idea of life and reality. It is no accident that Yeats's first performed play was called *The Land of Heart's Desire* or that the 'Father of the Irish Renaissance' was one Standish James O'Grady whose histories and prose romances assumed that Cuchulain was a real man living at an identifiable time and place in Ireland's distant past.

Yeats and George Russell (A. E.) believed that the old Celtic gods were returning to Ireland to bring about a spiritual renewal in a world that had been polluted by industrialism, commerce, materialism – everything summed up in the post-Darwinian concept of scientific rationalism. Ireland had been spared these movements; ancient, mystical beliefs about nature and the spirit world survived among the people, and were coming to life again with the re-discovery of Irish myth and legend in folk-tale and manuscript. In a letter of 1896 A. E. confided to Yeats: 'The gods have returned to Erin and have centred themselves in the sacred mountains and blow the fires through the country. They have been seen by several in vision, they will waken the magical instinct everywhere, and the universal heart of the people will turn to the old druidic beliefs. I note through the country the increased faith in faery things. The bells are heard from the mounds and sounding through the hollows of the mountains. A purple sheen in the inner air, perceptible at times in the light of day, spreads itself over the mountains. All this I can add my own testimony to.'[1]

The sincerity of A. E.'s belief is in no doubt – one had only to read his poetry or gaze at his pictures to share his sense of that mystical landscape. Yeats's stories in *The Secret Rose,* published in the following year, 1897, take us in a sweep through the past twenty centuries, dramatising the 'war of spiritual with natural order' and looking forward to a time when the spiritual forces of ancient Ireland will return in triumph to 'set up once more their temples of grey stone'. As Michael Robartes explains in the story 'Rosa Alchemica': 'Their reign has never ceased, but only waned in power a little for the Sidhe still pass in every wind, and dance and play at hurley, but they will not build their temples again till there have been martyrdoms and victories, and perhaps even that long-foretold battle in the Valley of the Black Pig.'[2]

These beliefs – for beliefs they were, not just whims or fancies – seem strange to us now. But there were all sorts of millennial doctrines in the air through the capitals of the world at the turn of the century, and heaven only knows what sort of weird prophesies will emerge out of Southern California as the year 2000 comes upon us. Theosophy, Rosicrucianism, Kabbalism, the Golden Dawn – the weird prophetic figure of Madame Blavatsky – pervaded the artistic salons of London,

Paris and Dublin, gained especial authority *here* because of the surviving Irish interest and belief in the Sidhe. The fever passed in a decade or so, and even while it lasted many of our writers viewed it sceptically. Looking at a picture by A. E., John Synge wrote:

> Adieu, sweet Angus, Maeve and Fand,
> Ye plumed yet skinny Sidhe,
> That poets played with hand in hand
> To learn their ecstasy.
>
> We'll stretch in Red Dan Sally's ditch,
> And drink in Tubber fair,
> And poach with Red Dan Philly's bitch,
> The badger and the hare.[3]

A generation later Louis MacNeice wrote:

> It's no go the Yogi-Man, it's no go Blavatsky,
> All we want is a bank balance and a bit of skirt in
> a taxi.[4]

But there is no doubt that the fairies and the ancient gods provided the Irish prose writer with a remarkable opportunity for experimental fiction, for breaking with the conventions of realism in pursuit of a purer sense of reality – or at the very least in pursuit of imaginative worlds, versions of Tír-na-nÓg, where some of the deeper and livelier human themes could be rehearsed and where we might for a while contemplate life as it could be rather than life as it is.

The main figures in this tradition of symbolic narrative were James Stephens, Eimar O'Duffy, Flann O'Brien, Austin Clarke and Mervyn Wall, and of course James Joyce himself who created the most monumental work of visionary prose in *Finnegans Wake* and deployed fable, myth and fantasy with such brilliant effect in, for instance, the 'Cyclops' scene in *Ulysses*. But as Joyce has had an essay to himself in this series I will merely *note* his contribution in the present context. I must also pass over writers whose main work is in different areas of literary creation – in realist fiction like Benedict Kiely, or in poetry and drama like Pádraic Colum – who have performed vividly but occasionally in the fabulous or fantastic: Mary Lavin in 'A Likely Story', Liam O'Flaherty in *The Dream* of Aengus, Tom MacIntyre in *The Charollais*, Seumas O'Kelly in *The Leprecaun of Kilmeen*, George FitzMaurice in *The Crows of Mefistopheles*, Brendan Kennelly in *The Crooked Cross*, Bryan MacMahon in his radiant idyll – recently reissued – *Children of the Rainbow*.

The first commanding figure therefore is James Stephens whose output involves six novels and three collections of short stories. Stephens is remarkable not only because of his readability and his perennial appeal to a wide audience, from children to adults, from academe to the common reader, but also for the many purposes served by his fictions – social commentary, mystical insight, philosophic discourse, prophesy, parody, satire. These themes and doctrines are not just tagged on to the fables but, for the most part, deftly embodied in plots and characterisations of great ingenuity and freshness where the reader may find in the words of C. S. Lewis 'some of the finest heroic narrative, some of the most disciplined pathos, and some of the cleanest prose which our century has produced.'[5]

Stephens's *annus mirabilis,* his year of miracle, was 1912, when he published his prose romance of Dublin, *The Charwoman's Daughter,* his first radical fantasy, *The Crock of Gold,* and his second volume of poetry, *The Hill of Vision.* He immediately became a best seller on both sides of the Atlantic, and *The Crock of Gold* has remained in print ever since – a distinction shared with few if any Irish works of fiction apart from Joyce's. The only rival I can think of in this respect is Somerville and Ross's *Irish R.M.* another book that has survived without the help of academe, finding, like *The Crock of Gold,* spontaneously, new readers in every generation.

The Crock of Gold has the typical Stephens blend and marriage of opposites: it is profound and funny, realistic and fabulous. Its cast of characters: the two crotchety Philosophers and their wives, Meehawl and his daughter, Caitilin, the Leprecauns of Gort na Cloca Mora, the policemen and the two gods, Pan and Angus Óg, make up a bizarre and visionary milieu, and their adventures between the malign city and the country of the gods have all the ingredients of suspense, surprise and comic reversal that make for a narrative cliffhanger. Then in the narrative pauses, as when Caitilin wanders drowsily through the pastures with her sheep and goats, or when the Philosopher broods disconsolately in prison, there is an enchanting sense of atmosphere that wooes the reader's mind towards the novel's governing themes. Finally there is the dialogue in which these themes are strenuously and divertingly argued. The god Pan, hairy and goat-legged, has come to Ireland and made off with Caitilin into the hills. Meehawl, her father, comes to the Philosopher who suggests that if all fails — and predictably it does — they can get Angus Óg, the Irish god of love, to intervene on their behalf. Meehawl likes the idea:

> 'He'd make short work of him, I'm thinking.'
> 'He might surely; but he may take the girl for himself all the same.'
> 'Well, I'd sooner he had her than the other one, for he's one of ourselves anyhow, and the devil you know is better than the devil you don't know.'
> 'Angus Óg is a god,' said the Philosopher severely.[6]

And so the two gods struggle for the love of Caitilin and for the mind of the Philosopher in the adventures that follow. It is of course a battle for the heart and mind of Ireland, a country where Victorian and Jansenist doctrines have subdued and enslaved the life-affirming values of Pan — erotic love and exuberance of the body — and outlawed the values of Angus, spiritual love and the poetic imagination. By the end of the book the battle has been won, and the fairy host sweeps down on the city to rescue the Philosopher, the Intellect of man, 'from the hands of the doctors and the lawyers, from the sly priests, from the professors whose mouths are gorged with sawdust, and the merchants who sell blades of grass' and return 'dancing and singing to the country of the gods. . .'[7]

The Crock of Gold is not only a universal fable of the war between the spiritual and the material, between instinct and law, love and convention, vision and reason, it is also a shrewd satire on Victorian Ireland which has become, as it were, a missionary country for Pan and his cult of love, passion, joy, spontaneity, the holiness of the heart's affections and the truth of imagination. Stephens is to that extent a faithful adherent of the Literary Revival as pioneered by Yeats and Russell, as ordained from the dawn of English Romanticism, in the visionary projections of Blake and Shelley.

But Stephens was his own man in one important respect. Where the older generation tended to view the Celtic gods and heroes with awe and reverence Stephens saw them with a kind of affectionate irony that made them amenable to his purposes as a satirist, a commentator on society's ill and humanity's failures in justice, compassion and vision.

In *The Demi-Gods* for instance, published in 1914 (the year of *Dubliners*) Stephens continued his fictional dialogue with eternity by bringing three angels with Irish names down on earth where they became part of the *entourage* of a tinker family, Patsy MacCann and his daughter Mary, with whom they travel the roads of Ireland. In the course of these wanderings they encounter a man called Brien O'Brien and the hero, Cuchulain, who is thrown out of heaven for stealing a three-penny piece, and who strips Mary MacCann of her clothes when he arrives naked on the Donnybrook Road. If Stephens outraged the spirit of O'Grady and Russell in making Cuchulain the first drag-artist in Irish fiction, he seems also to have provided an inspiration for some of the more experimental writers of the decade to follow.

Eimar O'Duffy's Cuchulain, when he comes on earth in *King Goshawk and the Birds,* goes one better on Stephens's hero by borrowing a body, that of a grocer's curate from Stoneybatter, one Robert Emmet Aloysius O'Kennedy. It is probably not a coincidence that O'Duffy situates his action in the area of Barney Kiernan's pub where the comic trans-formations of Joyce's *Cyclops* episode take place. And it is certainly not a coincidence that O'Duffy's chief character is, like Stephens's, a Philosopher with a capital P.

King Goshawk and the Birds is a more radical *satire* than anything in Stephens, where the satire tends to take second place to the comic and prophetic. *King Goshawk,* the first volume of a trilogy that foresees a world where capitalism is altogether rampant, and where the ruthless wheat magnate, King Goshawk, has not only enslaved humanity by 'selling blades of grass' on a large scale, but also captured for his wife, Guzzulinda, all the song-birds of the earth. It is to make war on that capitalist tyranny that Cuchulain is brought back, but

before the book's satire reaches out to its global significance
it is shrewdly deployed in the local cockpit of Dublin, Ireland's
capital city, now that the foreigner has been driven out.
O'Duffy had already written a bitter, sprawling novel, *The
Wasted Island*, on the events leading up to the Easter Rising –
he had taken the side of MacNeill against Pearse – and he was
not impressed with the narrow puritanism of the new state.

On his first day, therefore, Cuchulain, shackled uncomfortably within the decrepit body of O'Kennedy, responds
with heroic impetuosity to every sign of injustice, meanness
and inhospitality that he encounters. The collision between
heroic generosity and spontaneous passion on the one hand,
and bourgeois caution and prudery on the other, makes for
shrewd comedy and sharp social criticism. The hero, for
instance, outrages the sensibilities of a Drumcondra girl by
his overtures of heroic love: 'My desire is for two snowy
mountains, rose crowned, that are fenced about with thorns
and barriers of ice.'[8] He is treated as a sex maniac when he
tries to court a member of the local tennis club in similar vein,
and hauled before the censor. Though the book was published
two years before the Censorship of Publications Act it depicts
a world where the Arts are embattled: the nude 'was a
forbidden subject; and there had been a great holocaust of
existing works in this *genre* . . . two fifths of the world's
literature had suffered the same fate. . . The Old Testament
had been reduced to a collection of scraps, somewhat
resembling the Greek Anthology; and even the New
Testament had been purged of the plainer-spoken words of
Christ which were offensive to modern taste.'[9]

The ploy of bringing the hero into conjunction with the
unheroic present – skilfully used by Denis Johnston in his
play, *The Old Lady Says 'No'* – has its obvious satirical opportunities. Flann O'Brien, however, employs the device for
imaginary exploits and squalid adventures in the comic and
absurd in his strange fictional extravaganza, *At Swim-Two-
Birds*.

The book came out within a year of Beckett's first absurdist
novel, *Murphy*, and both fables – as if foreseeing the barbarism
of Hitler's war – have autistic heroes who retreat from reality
into their inner consciousness. Both works question the nature

of language by a radical approach to cliché. Kavanagh is soon to do the same in his doctrine of 'the habitual, the banal'.[10] Both ride roughshod over the conventions of the novel form.

Not only does O'Brien bring back Finn McCool to live in a Dublin pub in a milieu of assorted jocksers, but he assembles a Pooka, a Good Fairy, two cowboys, Conán Maol Mac Mórna and the medieval Mad Sweeney within his narrative patterns. Their works and days are inset to the story of an undergraduate at UCD who engages in spare-time literary activities of which they are the product. This technique of plot within plot, world within world, may well have been learned from James Stephens whom O'Brien openly admired. But the crabbed ingenuity of the humour is unique to O'Brien himself. Week after week through the war years that humour helped to keep Dublin sane, as it issued in *The Irish Times* under the pseudonym of Myles na Gopaleen.

The war itself prevented the publication of O'Brien's next and finest novel, a dark fantasy about earthly crime and eternal punishment called *The Third Policeman*. This masterpiece of comic macabre did not appear until 1967 when it made its author a sort of cult figure with connoisseurs of reflexive fiction. It was in *The Third Policeman* that O'Brien developed his 'atomic theory', that people who *rode* bicycles slowly *became* bicycles due to the interchange of atoms between man and vehicle. The theory becomes, in the novel, a sly mockery of Yeats and Joyce who based their late work on cyclical theories of human history. When O'Brien's hero wakes up in the afterlife he walks into a garda barracks and is greeted by the desk sergeant with the question, 'Is it about a bicycle?'[11] When the book's action has run its course we find the hero entering the same barracks and being greeted with the same question. His eternity is to be bound about a double wheel of fire.

If Stephens chose to bring the Gaelic heroes into a modern setting, Austin Clarke and after him, Mervyn Wall, chose to move modern Ireland back into the Middle Ages. Clarke's three prose romances, *The Bright Temptation* (1932), *The Singing Men at Cashel* (1937), and *The Sun Dances at Easter* (1952) are all chapters in what Clarke called 'the drama of racial conscience.'[12] Though they are set in medieval Ireland,

the world of Clarke's beloved Celtic Romanesque, these
fictions – like Clarke's medieval lyrics – are shrewdly relevant
to contemporary Ireland where Clarke sees a neurotic terror
of sexuality: there is the tormented anchorite, Malachi, in *The
Singing Men at Cashel,* and his voyeur's obsession with the
young queen; and that horrendous vision of Gleann Bolcan
in Kerry and its guilt-ridden inhabitants who have been
'crazied by scruples of conscience' to a hell of endless self-
abuse. Fantasy or fable, for Clarke, became in effect, a bleaker
form of psychological realism, a stage of history where the
main tensions in modern Irish life could be profiled in their
aboriginal simplicity. What was realist for Kiely and
McGahern was mystic in the narrative of Clarke.

Mervyn Wall, who moves two of his novels into the same
period and landscape, is more openly satirical in intention,
more thoroughly comic in his method. The eponymous hero
of *The Unfortunate Fursey* is a chubby little monk with a
stammer, living as a lay brother at Clonmacnoise. When the
devil and his army of evil spirits invest the monastery Fursey
is the only monk who cannot pronounce the words of
exorcism in time to repel their enchantments. The demons
camp in his cell and in time he is cast out upon the roads by
the abbot with Lucifer as his only friend and comforter. It is
part of Wall's purpose that the devil is by far the most attractive
figure on that medieval landscape. So much so that we tend
to applaud when at the Synod of Cashel he brings off a deal
that puts the Catholic clergy of Ireland in his bag for all time,
while he muses bleakly that hell will soon resemble an annual
general meeting of the Catholic Truth Society of Ireland. The
Devil has undertaken as his side of the bargain to rid Ireland
of the 'hideous sin of sex' – if the hierarchy agrees to turn a
blind eye on the others – 'simony, nepotism, drunkenness,
perjury and murder.'[13]

The clergy are thrilled with their side of the bargain, and
with Satan's summing up, in which he promises 'the clergy
of the country wealth and the respect of their people for all
time. When a stranger enters a village, he will not have to ask
which is the priest's house. It will be easy of identification,
for it will be the largest house there.'[14] This was 1946, and
though time has reversed the position both as regards sex and

priest's houses, the passage is grim witness to the spirit of the times, the sense of alienation felt by the writer in a society that banned his works and brought the weight of Church and State to bear on his every utterance.

In point of fact Mervyn Wall was one of the few Irish novelists never to be banned. There was no room for the sensual in his dry, cerebral humour, and the Censorship Board was after books that could be deemed 'indecent or obscene'. The mask of fantasy, however, enabled him to mock that system through the most wicked indirections. In *The Return of Fursey* he describes a Censor who arrives at Clonmacnoise to check out the library. Within three weeks he has committed to the flames many 'treasured manuscripts of secular and pagan origin. . . as well as four copies of the Old Testament, which he had denounced as being in general tendency indecent.'

> One of his principal qualifications for the post of Censor was that each of his eyes moved independently of the other, a quality most useful in the detection of hidden meanings. Sometimes one eye would stop at a word which might reasonably be suspected of being improper, while the other eye would read on through the whole paragraph before stopping and travelling backwards along the way it had come, until the battery of both eyes was brought to bear on the suspect word. Few words, unless their consciences were absolutely clear, could stand up to such scrutiny. . .'[15]

One could hardly find a more devastating image of sexual monomania then in this medieval Censor. And it is by going outside the conventions of realist fiction that the satiric vision of contemporary Irish society can be so sharply focused.

Mervyn Wall seems to be the last Irish writer to address himself seriously to this unserious mode of fiction. Benedict Kiely digressed brilliantly into it in *The Cards of the Gambler* where a folktale frames the destiny of a drunken Irish doctor. Tom MacIntyre's *The Charollais* looked like a brilliant sortie into the territory, but after its magical opening chapters it tended to lose impetus – and the author abandoned the form in favour of theatre and the short story. Brian Moore brought off one dashing *coup* in *The Great Victorian Collection,* but

returned immediately to the realist idiom. Alf MacLochlainn
has written a novella called *Out of Focus* (1977) which is
described by one critic as 'four short reflections on Flann
O'Brien's de Selby as dictated by Samuel Beckett.'[16] And there
was Bernard Share's *Inish* in 1966, weird and startling in its
ambition to monitor the quotidian chaos of an average
Irishman's mind, but somehow yielding to the chaos that it
had set out to dramatise. And there are the later experiments
of Desmond Hogan who has made a big reputation in Britain
for the manner in which he catches in refracted patterns the
nightmare of Irish history within ostensibly realist fiction.

With Mervyn Wall, however, the radical adventure of fable
and fantasy, the idiom of Stephens, O'Duffy and O'Brien,
tends to fade from Irish writing. Perhaps it has been replaced
by the more spectacular imaginings of science fiction – our
modern form of quest romance wherein technology caters for
the instinct once served by magic and miracle. Perhaps with
the retreat not only of superstition but of religion itself, heroes,
demons, fairies, gods and demi-gods have lost their hold on
the Irish imagination and faded into the light of common day.
I hope this is not the case. But even if it is we have still access
to a unique body of fiction in the dark and the light fantastic
to remind us of what we once had the impudence to imagine.

11. Samuel Beckett and the Protestant Ethic

Declan Kiberd

Samuel Barclay Beckett claims that he was born in Dublin on Good Friday 1906. His father was a flourishing quantity surveyor and his mother a devout Protestant housewife. That Good Friday fell, as fortune would have it, on April 13 and the symbolism was not lost on the future author. In his most famous play, *Waiting for Godot,* two tramps discuss the famous life that ended temporarily on Good Friday:

> VLADIMIR: But you can't go barefoot!
> ESTRAGON: Christ did.
> VLADIMIR: Christ! What's Christ got to do with it? You're not going to compare yourself to Christ!
> ESTRAGON: All my life I've compared myself to him.
> VLADIMIR: But where he lived it was warm, it was dry!
> ESTRAGON: Yes. And they crucified quick.[1]

Many of Beckett's characters ponder the inscrutable logic of God, as defined in the elegant formulation of St Augustine, who recalled the events surrounding that famous crucifixion: 'Do not despair; one of the thieves was saved. Do not presume; one of the thieves was damned. It's not a bad average.' Beckett insists that it is the shape of that sentence, rather than its religious message, which continues to captivate him in work after work. It isn't. As a writer, he is as religious as they come, a man whose entire *corpus* constitutes a latter-day *Book of Job*. Only one of the four evangelists speaks of a thief being saved, yet everybody chooses to believe that version, to the great amusement of Beckett and his tramps, who see such hopefulness as a sign of the inexplicable optimism of man.[2] A pessimist born on Friday the thirteenth might well wonder. Like all his major works, *Waiting for Godot* is a meditation on the problem of pain and suffering: why *was* one thief saved and the other damned? Beckett's prose works take up this attempt to study and fathom the mind of an inscrutable God, who feels no obligation to appear, much less to justify the apparent arbitrariness with which he has disposed of his favours. All of which gives rise to the paradox that Ireland's most famous nihilist may, in his intellectual concerns, be one of her most deeply religious writers.

Although religion has often been treated as a social force in the work of Joyce and O'Casey, it is fair to say that almost all our creative writers have been remarkably reluctant to admit questions of theology and belief as subjects befitting their art. Those who have satirised Catholicism have done so by pointing to its social effects: poverty accepted as the will of God, or to the suffering which a dogmatic code of elders may visit upon the sensitive young. There is much writing about religion in Ireland, but little truly religious writing, little spiritual probing in the literary form. This is hardly surprising. In a theocratic state where the nostrums of a single denominational faith are part of the very air one breathes, nobody discusses the spiritual content of religion, merely the social consequences. Those intellectuals brave enough to tackle the clergy on issues of spiritual principle have usually been political activists, such as James Connolly, who repeatedly pointed out to his Jesuit antagonists that a truth does not have to be couched in theological terms to be theologically true.[3] But, among our great writers, only Beckett has been courageous enough to write as if theology were too important to be left to the theologians; and, among our many major artists of Protestant background, he is the first since Swift to confront head-on the great drama of the puritan conscience, tackling such themes as work and reward, anxious self-scrutiny, the need for self-reliance and the distrust of artifice and even art. His work seems like an answer to George Bernard Shaw's prayer for a truly Protestant writer who would demonstrate that 'Protestantism is a great historic movement of Aspiration, Reformation and Self-Assertion against spiritual tyranny rather than that organisation of false gentility which often takes its name in vain in Ireland.'[4]

The piety of his devout mother did not recommend itself to the young Sam Beckett, who found Irish Protestantism lacking in spiritual depth, a mere matter of tennis-clubs and water-biscuits. On the death of his parents, according to Deirdre Bair's biography, he complained that the faith offered no more consolation than an old school tie.[5] All of his early prose works are filled with ferocious assaults on the Protestant ethic of effort, work and inevitable reward. The very title of his first collection of stories, *More Pricks Than Kicks,* is an obscene pun on a passage from the Protestant Bible so beloved of his mother.[6] This was enough to have the book banned by the censors in Ireland and placed by Mrs Beckett on the highest shelf in the family home, well out of the sights of curious visitors. The hero of these stories is the sinfully indolent Belacqua, so named after the character in Dante who lazily deferred his repentance until the last possible moment, and was therefore condemned to wait at the foot of Mount Purgatory, enduring the same span of time in waiting as he had once passed in indolence. This is intended by Dante as a punishment, but for Beckett it is a liberation, since Belacqua aspires to nothing more than the praise of idleness. He is 'a dirty low-down low Church Protestant high-brow' in flight from the world of work, like the young Beckett who resigned his post as Trinity College and confessed to his bemused friends that he wanted instead to lie on his back and fart and think about Dante. 'What I am on the look-out for,' says Belacqua, 'is nowhere, as far as I can see.' And so he prefers to stay in bed, curled up in the foetal position adopted by his Danteesque exemplar.

Yet Belacqua's declaration of war upon the work-ethic is couched in decidedly Protestant terms, as the inevitable outcome of his desire for self-sufficiency in the world of pure mind. 'The mind at last its own asylum,' he muses longingly, in a near-parody of a famous passage in *the* great Protestant epic of Milton:

> A mind not to be changed by place or time.
> The mind is its own place, and in itself,
> Can make a Heav'n of Hell, a Hell of Heav'n.

(That Satan should have spoken these deathless lines merely shows that Milton's devil is a Protestant.) Yet Belacqua fails this test, for 'his anxiety to explain himself constituted a break-down in the self-sufficiency which he never wearied of arrogating to himself.' He fondly imagines himself to be an indolent bohemian, but at heart he is a puritan, seeking to replace the smooth Catholic rituals of the aesthetic adventure with a more literal-minded low church honesty. He is, in fact, an anti-bohemian, who rejects the elegant vestments of a Wilde and dons the hair-shirt of the puritan, deliberately wearing his hair like stubble. 'Here again,' says the narrator, 'in his plumping for the austerity of a rat's back, he proclaimed himself in reaction to the nineties.'[7] His style spurns the careless ease of that decade in a wilful celebration of awkwardness: 'with a lotion that he had he had given alertness to the stubble.'[8] At times, even the narrative trips over itself in its cultivation of linguistic misfortune. Our hero downs a bottle of alcohol, but without panache, and 'the effect of this was to send what is called a glow of warmth what is called coursing through his veins.'[9] The constant jagged interventions by the pedantic narrator, along with the fussy cross-references in footnotes, increase the pains of the reader, who is never long allowed to indulge his suspension of disbelief. This happens repeatedly in Beckett's plays, too, which constantly are interrupted with the reminder that they are only plays, making no serious attempt to compete with reality. By breaking the dramatic illusion, to assert the actor's self at the expense of his role, these plays articulate the puritan case against *mimesis* in art and remind us of the common puritan fear that the integrity of the self is violated by play-acting. With these endless interruptions, Beckett's plays are a slow-motion re-enactment of the puritan closing-down of the theatres. Moreover, his stages are stripped of all unnecessary props, like bleak low-church altars. The famous aphorism 'No symbols were none intended' seems, in this context, less an attack on the army of literary critics than on the ultra-Catholic symbolists of the 1890s. It is an apology for the honest awkwardness of his prose, its refusal to settle into a facile style. This is not an art which will erode the integrity of the self, but one which will remind every man how difficult and painful it is to impersonate his own self, much less anybody else's.

So the awkward style embodies for the reader the book's puritan theme that only by our sufferings do we achieve any importance or convince ourselves that we exist. Belacqua crawls cruciform along the ground beside Trinity College, and strangely enjoys the pain of the rain beating against his exposed body, just as he likes to squeeze the boil on his neck, because the ensuing pain is 'a guarantee of identity'. Yet the meaning of pain eludes him. He feels sympathy for Jonah in the whale, for the condemned killer McCabe, for the live lobster in the boiling pot – but still he lashed into the lobster for dinner. 'Well, it's a quick death, God help us all,' he muses in self-justification, but it is not.[10]

For Beckett's earliest heroes, the most protracted crucifixion of all is the life of men doomed to earn their living by the sweat of their brows. They may be in reaction against the indolent nineties, but not entirely. So the novel *Murphy* has been well described by Dylan Thomas as a combination of Sodom and Begorrah. There is a Wildean touch about many of the one-liners. 'You saved my life,' says Neary accusingly to a friend, 'now palliate it.'[11] To Murphy the raising of Lazarus seemed perhaps the one occasion on which the Messiah had overstepped the mark,[12] a line reminiscent of Wilde's grief-stricken young man who explained his tears to Jesus: 'Lord, I was dead and you brought me back to life. What else can I do but weep?' This *fin-de-siècle* languor is one of the factors in Murphy's *accidie,* but a deeper explanation lies in his conviction that the world of work would prevent him coming alive in the mind. His girl-friend Celia begins to understand that 'a merely indolent man would not be so affected by the prospect of employment', that at the root of Murphy's refusal of the shallow Protestant ethic is a deeply Protestant desire to unlock and inhabit his own mind. Soon, she too 'cannot go where livings are made without feeling that they were being made away.'[13] So she stops pacing her beat as a prostitute in the market, 'where the frenzied justification of life as an end to means threw light on Murphy's prediction, that livelihood would destroy life's goods.'[14] Murphy hates the work-ethic, as an end to means and an obsession with ends. Hence his assertion of the higher morality of play, the one occasion on which human beings engage in goal-free activities, when they are happy with something as means rather than end.

In this random world, Murphy plays a game of chance. It is pure chance that causes Celia to meet him at the start and

pure chance that kills him in the end. Events have no meaning
– they simply happen. The climax of the book is a chess-game.
Hence, too, the playful ruse by which he defrauds a vested
interest 'to the honourable extent of paying for one cup of tea
and consuming 1.83 cups approximately.'[15] In a world devoid
of meaning, identity comes only from the contemplation of
objects in permutation.

The fraud in the restaurant is a hilarious contemporary spoof
on the socially-committed literature of the nineteen-thirties
when the book was written, but it is even more urgently an
attack on the notion of the inherent dignity of work. The
waitress, 'a willing little bit of sweated labour', knows that
the customer is paying five times the true cost of his meal and
so deems it reasonable 'to defer to his complaints up to but
not exceeding 50% of his exploitation.'[16] The narrator asks us
to ponder the immense implications of the incident and to
compare the belligerents – on the one side, a colossal league
of plutocratic caterers, on the other, a seedy solipsist with
fourpence.[17] Murphy's contempt for the waitress is based on
her acquiescence within a system of 'pensums and prizes' to
which he feels wholly indifferent. 'What was all working for
a living but a procuring and a pimping for the money-bags,
so that they might breed?' he asks. And the entire book is an
indictment of those smug souls, like the landlady Miss
Carridge, who sits 'with the conviction of having left undone
none of those things that paid and done none of those things
that did not pay.'[18]

It takes Murphy a lifetime to learn that he cannot offload
responsibility for himself onto others. Even in the mental
hospital, he compounds his earlier sin by seeking an image of
absolute self – sufficiency in the patients, i.e. in other people.
Only at the very end does he live the life of a man who knows
that he must no longer follow the astrology of Pandit Suk.
'They were *his* stars, he was the prior system.' To that limited
extent, he becomes a hero who stands for an extreme self-
reliance, one of those rare characters who, in Beckett's own
words, 'will not allow their systems to be absorbed in the
cluster of a greater system.'[19] For all their veneer of decadence,
there is something strangely puritanical about such indolent
heroes as Balacqua and Murphy, a reflection, perhaps, of their

youthful author who confessed to Thomas MacGreevy that an inherited streak of puritanism was 'the straightforward and dominant part of his personality'. [20] This withdrawal into a pose of wounded superiority, of arrogant and lonely otherness, was later denounced by Beckett as a morbid negation of life by a stuck-up prig who felt himself too good for anything else.

The heroes who succeed Murphy in Beckett's trilogy have none of his arrogance, but they are even more puritanical in their penchant for remorseless self-scrutiny, and in their dismissal of good works and charity. Moreover, they seem to bespeak a return on the part of their author to an even more frankly Protestant conception of art as testimony. The trilogy includes a hilarious spoof on the pedantic legalities of the Catholic sacrament of confession, but its monologues represent an eloquent endorsement of a confessional art. The Catholic confession is a ritual conversation, brought to a satisfactory conclusion in the absolution administered by the priest. But, by contrast, the Protestant confession is made finally to oneself ('every man his own priest') in the form of a monologue which is, by definition, unending – a point made by Hugh Kenner in his brilliant guide to the works of Beckett. No wonder that Beckett told John Montague, a poet reared in a Catholic tradition, 'what you need is monologue', [21] for in the trilogy that form dramatises what Kenner has called the 'issueless Protestant confrontation with conscience'. [22] It may not be entirely accidental that Yeats (another writer schooled in Protestant values) should have defined poetry in somewhat similar terms as 'a quarrel with the self'; or that the plays of Seán O'Casey, a working-class Protestant, are all grounded in the moral value of self-responsibility, exemplified, most notably and least expectedly in the loyalist slut, Bessie Burgess. If Joyce remained obsessed with the symbols and themes of the faith which he professed to reject, then it may well be that the interest of Yeats, O'Casey and Beckett in the ethical dilemmas of Protestantism did not end with their abandonment of the Church of Ireland.

The confessional nature of the trilogy is confirmed by Beckett, who says that he conceived its first book *Molloy* on the day when he became aware of his past stupidity in not writing out of personal experience, in his refusal to 'accept

the dark side as the commanding side of my personality'.[23]
This last phrase might be an inadvertant summary of the 'plot'
of *Molloy,* which chronicles the attempt by the prim, bourgeois Catholic Moran to confront the primeval Molloy within,
to locate the panting anti-self that struggles to emerge,
divesting Moran of his illusions, of property, industry,
purpose, and, above all, religious belief. Where this
uncovering of the anti-self is for Yeats an artistic imperative,
it has for Beckett all the confessional qualities of a religious
testimony, a point conceded in the trilogy when the author
protests that he has no intention, even at this advanced stage,
of giving way to literature. The works must be taken as
testimony, or not at all. The stop-start sentences of the
monologues emphasise the puritan expenditure of energy that
went into their writing, and the heroic qualities of self-reliance
and endurance required also of the committed reader.

The logical result of Protestantism is the death of God, or
so the trilogy would claim. The virtue of self-reliance, if taken
to its conclusion, can have only this result, for man is always
'the prior system'. Moran begins as a devout believer in God
and externally-sanctioned systems, but soon he is a prey to
doubt; 'and if I had not hastily sunk back into my darkness I
might have gone to the extreme of conjuring away the chief
too and regarded myself as solely responsible for my wretched
existence.'[24] By the end, he has achieved that freedom in the
mind and can listen instead to an inner voice, which relies on
no vengeful deity to make itself heard. With this voice, he can
liberate Molloy, unchain his innermost self, confess and
thereby expiate the sins of the past. Moreover, the man who
once 'found it painful not to understand' can now accept the
incomprehensible patterns of dancing bees. Part of the comfort
is the knowledge that the patterns are an impermeable closed
system of their own and that therefore he will not be tempted
to offload responsibility for himself onto them: 'And I would
never do my bees the wrong I had done my God, to whom
I had been taught to ascribe my angers, fears, desires, and
even my body.'[25] Indeed, all through the book we encounter
suggestions that all forms of authority – whether God, fathers
or systems of belief – induce mindlessness and loss of
responsibility in their subjects. For example, Moran's son

always loses his way when accompanied by his father, but survives handsomely when left in charge of himself.[26] This applies even more significantly to the narrator, who seems to grow in stature and authority as the trilogy progresses and who tries harder and harder to reach the very bedrock of his personality. The constant finicky adjustments of imprecise words may be seen in this light not as mockeries of language, but as attempts by the testifier to assume full responsibility for his chosen idioms. If the narrator of the trilogy emerges as its hero, albeit one who never does plumb the authentic unconscious, its comic butts are those members of the hard-working bourgeoisie who seek in the boredom of daily routine to escape from the suffering of being. Beckett offers a ferocious satire on the Saposcat family whose life is full of axioms – the criminal absurdity of a garden without roses, or a family without a son going on for the liberal professions.

By the end of the second volume *Malone Dies,* the code of austere self-responsibility to which the narrator aspires is broken and Macmann entrusts himself to an asylum whose officials advise him: 'Take no thought for anything. It is we shall think and act for you from now forward.'[27] Worse still is the recognition that God himself is not a Protestant but a highly irresponsible fellow, who 'does not seem to need reasons for doing what he does, and for omitting to do what he omits to do, to the same degree as his creatures.'[28] But the unkindest cut of all comes in the third and final volume *The Unnamable,* where the Protestant notion of the pensum, the labour imposed as a punishment for having been born with original sin, is revealed as a mere illusion, concocted by timid men to confer a bogus meaning on their lives: 'All this business of a labour to accomplish before I can end. I invented it all, in the hope it would console me.'[29] But there is no consolation – merely the knowledge that Protestantism has ceased to be a potent myth and become a self-confessed fiction.

None of Beckett's prose writings after the trilogy carries these insights any further. That would be too much to expect, since Beckett has already taken us to the very edge of religious knowledge. For the Protestant ethic of work, he has substituted the Puritan ethic of relentless self-exploration, and produced the most striking testimony of our times to the need

for human sufferings to be at once experienced and unex-
plained.

Those who may continue to question this account of Beckett
as a puritan testifier are urged to look once more at the nearest
available photograph of Ireland's greatest living author.

12. The Short Story after the Second World War

John Jordan

During the decade after the Second World War, if asked to name the practising masters of the Irish short story, this reader would have had to tick off the Aran Islander, Liam O'Flaherty and the Corkmen, Sean O'Faolain and Frank O'Connor.[1] On reflection he would have added Elizabeth Bowen, Michael McLaverty, Mary Lavin and Bryan MacMahon. Of these last only MacMahon from Listowel, County Kerry, had published his first collection after the war. His stories had first come to prominence in *The Bell*. *The Lion Tamer* (1948) was followed by *The Red Petticoat* (1955). In this last collection, 'Exile's Return' belies its conventional title, which suggests a reversion to older writers, as far back as George Moore, but sounds a peal of loving-kindness in a man of barbarian instincts, a significant contrast to O'Flaherty primitives. But *The Red Petticoat* was overshadowed in critical esteem by the first collection of another *Bell* writer, James Plunkett from Dublin whose collection, *The Trusting and the Maimed* first appeared in New York in 1955. It contained ten stories. In 1977 his *Collected Stories* appeared, containing the original volume and eight additional stories. Twenty-odd years later the impact of the earlier stories had not lessened, notably in 'The Trusting and the Maimed' and 'The Eagles and the Trumpets'. Plunkett has remained a phenomenon in the Irish short story. In a good deal of his work he celebrates and laments with both the working and the lower middle classes of Dublin City. Joyce had of course done this, but with rather less empathy where the depressively unimpassioned native brand of Jansenism is concerned. But since Plunkett is an artist, the effect is not one of depression but one of purgative sadness, not seldom something more, as in 'The Trusting and the Maimed' where the doom of a wounded pigeon and the putative doom of an office worker with an unwanted pregnancy are juxtaposed. One passage may serve to illustrate the story's arid pain, its bleak irony. The girl Rita returns to her family home, faced with informing her parents that she is pregnant. She has rejected the option of abortion and is taking the advice of a confessor. At home she hears a murmuring of voices which she seems to recognise. (I quote.) 'She repeated to herself: "He said you're to forgive me, that God has already forgiven me. He said to tell you. He said God has forgiven me and that's why I am to tell you that if God has forgiven me you are to forgive me too."'[2] And later: 'She flung open the front room door. It took her some time to realise that the murmuring had not been in her head. Her father and mother and her two youngest brothers and sisters were all on their knees. Her mother looked around first. They were saying the family rosary.'[3] It is almost a moment of pity and terror. We never learn how Rita's parents will react to the news. Yet there is the terrible implication that fervent and formal familial piety may be utterly detached from the exercise of compassion, even within the family circle. But my own favourite Plunkett story is one of the additional stories in *Collected Stories*. 'A Walk Through the Summer', about the encounter between one of Plunkett's many young white-collar workers and a particularly unappealing blind man, on a summer's evening in the Ballsbridge area. Plunkett has always been partial to symbolic personages after the style of the old man with 'redrimmed horny eyes' whose image Joyce so much fears in *A Portrait of the Artist as a Young Man*. Plunkett's 'blind man' is the very embodiment of what he sees in his countrymen of bigotry, chauvinism, and self-righteous obscurantism. Lack of sight is perhaps too obvious a physical emblem. But the emblem is less important than the several epiphanies of Tom Moore's (for such is his name) spiritual torpor and congenital spite. When Sara, a Polish refugee who has lost her family in the war, admits that if offered meat on a Friday she would probably eat it, blind Tom Moore responds with racially symptomatic smugness: 'Foreign Catholics is notorious luke-warmers. They're not a patch on Irish Catholics. The Pope himself said that.'[4] The blind man's frightful parroting of political clichés and homiletic clap-trap counterpoints a story of adultery in the mind. Perhaps Mr Plunkett is in the line of Sean O'Faolain in his treatment of adulterous affairs, always compassionate but never dispensing absolutely with the traditional moral code.

In those years after the war the percipient were aware of another *Bell* writer, Seamus de Faoite, from Kerry (1915–1980) whose only collection, *The More We Are Together* did not appear until shortly after his death. Benedict Kiely has described him as a 'supreme raconteur'.[5] He is also a supreme, if sometimes over-roseate, chronicler of his home-town Old Killarney. Not perhaps the best but certainly the most characteristic story in his small collection is 'The Old Stock' with its tender evocation of a dying world of traditional trades and tradesmen. And it is arguable that de Faoite has more control over his highly-coloured prose than, for example, his fellow-countyman, Bryan MacMahon or the next writer to be noted in this survey, Benedict Kiely from County Tyrone. MacMahon, de Faoite and Kiely belong to a tradition of Irish writing, diffuse, picaresque, anecdotal, which goes back to the last century and the so-called Handy-Andy school. Kiely certainly, with a great deal more sophistication and taste, may find his literary ancestry as much in Samuel Lover and Charles Lever as in the nowadays more respectable, viewed artistically, William Carleton. Kiely had published seven novels before his first collection of stories, *A Journey to the Seven Streams* (1963). A second collection was *A Ball of Malt and Madame Butterfly* (1973) and a third, *A Cow in the House* (1978). A year before the last-named he published *Proxopera,* described as a novel, but two years later, in an American collection, as a *novella*. It might have been included as a very long 'short story' in the *Cow in the House* volume. It must be considered in a short story context for it is evidence of how far Kiely can extend the form, as well as for its uncharacteristically elegant shape and its acerbity of feeling. Written 'In Memory of the Innocent Dead' its indictment of mindless terrorism cuts across the usually genial, even complaisant, Kiely of the other shorter fictions. Formally it belongs with Brian Moore from Belfast and his *Catholics* (1972) and *The Newton Letter* (1982) of John Banville from Dublin. The three fictions provide models for Irish short story writers, who lack the material or the stamina for the novel.

As indicated above, Benedict Kiely is in the *seanachaí* tradition, complete with digressions and diversions. At their best, these exercises in sheer story-telling, with their heavy stress on nostalgia and the transience of youth and physical beauty, and the chasm of the tomb, bring us into an extraordinary peopled world. It is also a world where the strands of Irish Catholicism and Irish paganism, of Irish piety and Irish superstition, are inextricably intermingled. The folk-element may be seen uppermost in stories like 'The Dogs in the Great Glen' and 'God's Own Country' from the first and second collections respectively. In the last-named, a dyspeptic hack journalist is transmuted into a healthy and confident professional man by a trip to a western island. Significantly, his rehabilitation is brought about quite as much by an act of generosity to a tormenting colleague as by a half-tumbler of a bishop's whiskey, as much by benevolence as by barley. The folk element in Kiely is accentuated by his acute sense of place and the associations, historical-pastoral-comical, of the remotest nooks in, if not the whole island, his own county and province. Anecdotage, topography and pawky humour are the makings of the title story in *A Journey*. The special Kiely earthiness can be heavy-handed as in the title story of *A Ball of Malt* but redeemed by sad lyricism and a sense of the burden of time as in 'The Green Lanes' from the same volume. I have mentioned Carleton, Lover and Lever in connection with Kiely. It might be more apposite to invoke the Somerville and Ross of *The Irish R.M.* crossed with the *Sportsman's Sketches* of Turgenev.

Two other writers who began to publish collections of short stories comparatively late in life are Patrick Boyle from Antrim and Terence de Vere White from Dublin. The former's *At Night All Cats are Grey* came in 1966, followed by *All Looks Yellow to the Jaundiced Eye* (1969) and *A View from Calvary* (1976). Boyle, it seems to me, was the Irish writer closest to the naturalist tradition of Emile Zola, as may be seen in a story like 'Blessed are the Meek' from his first collection. Yet he also may owe much to Liam O'Flaherty, especially when his stories depend on close observation of animals, as in 'Meles Vulgaris' from the second collection.

Terence de Vere White published ten novels before his collection of stories, *Big Fleas and Little Fleas* (1976). De Vere White is very much at home in clubs and restaurants and offices and drawing-rooms. Like the character in 'Lunch with Tom' he might say, 'I grew up knowing everybody'.[6] Yet he can achieve, as in 'Cake on Sunday', ironic poignancy in the treatment of commonplace material, in this case, an employer-spinster-secretary relationship.

Another *Bell* writer, Anthony C. West from County Down published a collection in America, *River's End* (1958) of which the title story, reprinted in a recent selection deserves to be better known (as does all his work) for its depiction of teenage and adult sexuality in a Protestant North of Ireland rural community. Such a story serves to redress the imbalance in the Irish short story whereby sexual repression or distortion might seem to be peculiarly Irish Catholic problems. West might certainly be accused of unduly lush descriptive writing, but not of insensitivity to the traumata of the adolescent and the prematurely aged.

The stories of William Trevor from County Cork, like those of his fellow Cork writer, Elizabeth Bowen, are only minimally set in Ireland. His 'Irish Stories' have been assembled in *The Distant Past* (1979). Of his five original collections, perhaps the best known in this country is *The Ballroom of Romance* (1972) by virtue of the title story's success as a television play. Mr Trevor's touch in handling Irish material is almost always sure (in this being akin to Bowen) despite his English residence. 'The Ballroom of Romance' has an awesome authenticity. Its shabby immortal longings have the faintly acid fragrance of a latter-day Chekov. Not unfairly, one may say that this little masterpiece might not have been written without the precedents of O'Faolain and O'Connor. But in a story like 'Death in Jerusalem' (from *Lovers in their Time* [1978]) he rivals O'Faolain in the magnanimous incisiveness of his Catholic clerical portraiture. Rather remarkably so, given his Church of Ireland background.

Examples of Irish novelists who also practise the short story are not uncommon. But there are also dramatists who have distinguished themselves in the *genre*. A very special case is Brendan Behan, of course, from Dublin. Three widely dis-

parate stories have survived which are of sufficiently liigh
quality to suggest the futile hypothesis that his energy and
garrulousness needed the discipline of short fiction. These
stories, which have been included in Peter Fallon's edition of
After the Wake (1981), a collection of uncollected and
unpublished prose pieces, are 'A Woman of No Standing'
(1950), a taut vignette of the position of 'the other woman' at
a working-class funeral, 'After the Wake' (1950), a pioneer
insight into Dublin working-class homosexuality, and 'The
Confirmation Suit' (1950), in which there is a magistral
triumph of pathos over sentimentality.

Another successful dramatist, and also novelist, Walter
Macken (1915-1968) from Galway City left three collections,
of which the last was published posthumously: *The Colly Doll*
(1969). It contains eight ungathered stories and thirteen from
his first collection *The Green Hills* (1956). Macken's stories
are in the main light-weight and conventional. But they are,
within their limits, a kind of counterbalance to the more
sombre western vision of O'Flaherty and Ó Cadhain.

A much more distinguished dramatist, Brian Friel, like
Benedict Kiely, from Omagh, County Tyrone, has published
two collections, *The Saucer of Larks* (1962) and *The Gold in
the Sea* (1966). Friel, underrated as a short story writer, is
gentle and elegiac in tone. 'Mr Sing My Heart's Delight', from
the first collection, the study of an exquisite human contact
between an old Irish-speaking Donegal woman and a young
Indian pedlar, may say more about community relations and
racial tensions than a parcel of White Papers.

I must note also that yet another important dramatist,
Eugene McCabe, born in Glasgow but of Monaghan
background, has published one collection, *Heritage* (1978). Of
the six long stories, the title-piece, almost long enough to
make a *novella* deserved far more attention than it received,
for its unblinking insight into the tribal hatreds of South
Fermanagh. The tale is told from the point of view of a young
Protestant farmer, a member of the UDR, from a family split
by tolerance of, and hatred and fear of, Papists. Like Anthony
C. West's 'River's End' it reminds us that a narrow and joyless
view of sex may be the greatest common bond between large
sections of the Protestant and Catholic communities in

Northern Ireland, unless it be that the cult of vengeance is an even greater one.

The 1960s brought a succession of collections which might be said to have changed not alone the range of the Irish short story but the modes of style and the tones of voice. From the publication of *Felo de Se* by Aidan Higgins (1960), the drift towards cosmopolitanism as the norm rather than the exception, is noticeable. Mr Higgins's six long short stories are set variously in Ireland, England, Germany and South Africa. Although clearly there are signs of influence from Beckett and the Argentinian Borges (though not as to the brevity in the latter case) it seems to me that the dominant influence may be Djuna Barnes, the American novelist and short story writer, through her stories in *A Book* (1923) and her novel *Nightwood* (1936). His style even may be influenced by Barnes's: crabbed and damasked, gnomic and oblique, unabashedly learned. Barnes's style and much else from Barnes may be found in a story like 'Lebensraum', for the Wandering Fraulein, Sevi Klein, pushing forty, has much in common with Robin Vote, the expatriate American girl in *Nightwood*. And Robin's relationship with husband and lovers is as remote and as scorching as Sevi's with her Irish lover, 'the doubtful product of Jesuit casuistry and the Law School'.[7] But the close of the story suggests not Barnes but the Joyce of the 'Nausicaa' section in *Ulysses*.

In 1964, John Montague , born in the USA but of Tyrone parentage and ancestry, had already established a reputation as a poet, when he published *Death of a Chieftain*. Predictably, his stories have images meet for verse and symbolic patterns. The cosmopolitan note tinkles clearly. In 'An Occasion of Sin' French feminine urbanity confronts Irish prurience, absurd and piteous. The title story is set in Mexico, in a town peopled with Graham Greene-ish figures, except for the protagonist, self-described as 'a renegade Ulster Presbyterian',[8] a drunken archaeologist who dreams of linking Newgrange with the Aztecs' burial chambers. Bernard Corunna Coote is an extraordinarily rich emblem of Irish Orangery's complexity.

In 1968, Edna O'Brien from Clare, already a best-selling novelist, produced her first collection, *The Love Object*, followed by *A Scandalous Woman* (1974). The title story of the first is Ms O'Brien, the *faux-naïve* amorist, at her most tedious but the title story of the second, set in her native county, is poignant, bitter and often very funny, despite the narrator's reflection that 'ours indeed was a land of shame, a land of murder and a land of strange sacrificial women.' In this book other stories show some of the less publicised aspects of Ms O'Brien's talents, notably 'The Favourite', about a 'sacrificial woman' killed with kindness, and 'The Creature', an essay in unmixed compassion, about a lost mother and lost son. Also in 1968, Julia O'Faolain, from Dublin, produced her first collection, *We might See Sights!*, followed by *Man in the Cellar* (1974). In the first, her scope includes a kind of student life circling around University College, Dublin (in the early fifties) which might well be compared with that to be found in *A Portrait* and Flann O'Brien's *At Swim-Two-Birds,* set in the early 1900s and early 1930s respectively. In this context should be read 'First Conjugation', 'A Pot of Soothing Herbs' and 'Chronic'. In the second collection, stories are set variously in Ireland, England, France, Italy, America and sixth-century Gaul ('This is My Body' is the seed of Ms O'Faolain's astonishing Gaulish novel *Woman in the Wall* [1975]). From the second collection, 'I Want us to be in Love' and 'A Travelled Man' both illustrate Ms O'Faolain's abiding fascination with abrasive cultures. In the first, a middle-class English teenager is caught between the functional sex offered by her Franco-American lover, all commitment and computers, and the romantic trappings of the very elderly desire of his father, all champagne and Chevalier. In the second, two Italians, a middle-aged hired archivist and a girl sent 'to learn the language', are thrown together in the home of a Californian professor of the history of art and his wife; the old Henry Jamesian vision of the American innocent abroad in the European sea of corruption and subtlety now scarcely obtains. Rather we have European innocents being 'educated' in the vagaries of psychoanalytically-geared American society. One must add that James would not have seen anything 'fine' in Ms O'Faolain's sexual frankness. But she well knows how American academics can talk, whatever they do.

Tom MacIntyre from Cavan, brought us into an emotional territory of what might be called obliquity, but which I would prefer to call caution, with his collection *Dance the Dance* (1970) followed only recently by *The Harper's Turn* (1982), which contains work written much earlier. In the earlier volume, 'The Bracelet' in very little space rings a change on the theme of the visiting aunt from the States. MacIntyre's hesitant style precludes judgment on the exact nature of Auntie May's resentment over an unreturned bracelet. Surprisingly, Henry James again comes to mind. In the second volume, a story like 'Boarding' evokes with teasing ambiguity the whole history of a great boarding school run by an Order. 'Stallions' is an entirely original gloss on the hoary theme of Irish puritanism in relation to not only sexual pleasure but procreation itself.

Coincidently, MacIntyre's contemporary John McGahern, born in Dublin but of Leitrim-Roscommon background, must also be hailed for the cautious vision. This is not immediately patent in his first collection *Nightlines* (1970). But the cosmopolitan, or rather international key is there. Possible American exile and consequent conscription intrude in 'Korea' into the already uneasy relationship between father and son. In his second collection, *Getting Through* (1974), 'Along the Edges' points to McGahern's pre-occupation with the notion that Auden's injunction is not enough: we must love one another *and* die, daily. This metaphysical idea of love, emotional and carnal, also permeates 'Doorways' and 'Sierra Leone'. In the latter the Irish lovers are surely exceptional in their awareness of the Cuban Crisis. After the Russian ships have lain off Cuba, the narrator reflects: 'The morning met me as other damp cold Dublin mornings, the world almost restored to the everyday. The rich uses we dreamed last night when it was threatened that we would put it to if spared were now forgotten, when again it lay all about us with such tedious abundance.'[9] McGahern's streak of Manichaeism is in that last phrase. The cosmopolitan note sounds loudly and desolately in 'The Beginning of an Idea', the story of a Finnish theatre woman obsessed with the death of Chekov and her adventures in Andalusia under the Franco regime. Unlikely as it may seem, McGahern's style reminds me of the famous 'dryness' aimed at by Stendhal. It well suits the cautious vision.

Val Mulkerns from Dublin, although she published two

novels in her twenties, did not publish a collection of stories until 1978. *Antiquities* is to a degree experimental, in that the stories are interlocked over a period of three generations from 1916 to the early seventies. The recording generation is a youngish matron who either in the first or third person figures in seven out of the ten stories. The tone throughout is cool but not unimpassioned, if the instinct to express restrained grief and unsavage indignation be a kind of passion, as when she touches on neo-republicanism, in 'The Four Green Fields', and 'The Touch', a story which though it caused no stir, encapsules more than one aspect of the Northern Ireland cataclysm. In other stories she deals with relatively humdrum domestic issues, though 'France is So Phoney' goes outside the usual run of Irish fiction in its acknowledgement of male marital frigidity. Ms Mulkerns's second collection, *An Idle Woman* (1980), has the same virtues of coolness and contained regret. But she covers new ground, especially in 'Memory and Desire', an elegiac study of an abandoned husband's dangerous tenderness for a young male TV producer. Ms Mulkerns's treatment of this difficult theme underlines the creative force of understatement.

The late seventies and early eighties saw a plethora of collections, due largely, but not exclusively, to the enterprise of the Poolbeg Press. From now on, reference must depend on personal preference rather than attempted inclusiveness. 1976 saw two volumes which demonstrate admirably the survival of traditional form, and the burgeoning of forms both experimental and poetic. Maeve Kelly from Limerick has familiar rural and provincial themes, and close attention to the picturesque in the natural world in her *A Life of Her Own*, but a story like 'The False God' has an unusual tartness plus a dash of grotesquerie. Ms Kelly has an unexploited vein.

But there is nothing conventional in *Night in Tunisia* by Neil Jordan from Sligo/Dublin. 'Sand', an intuition of the mysteries of pubertial sexuality, male and female, has something of the quality of a blue Picasso; 'A Bus, a Bridge, a Beach' and 'The Old-Fashioned Lift' suggest the influence of Alain Robbe-Grillet and the *nouveau roman*, though their style has its own bleak poetry. Jordan may also, like another innovator, Aidan Higgins, nearly twenty years earlier, be influenced by Beckett.

In *Sixpence in Her Shoe* (1977) Maura Treacy from Kilkenny brings us back again to pastoral Ireland. Her stories are usually but effectively inconclusive. An especially fine instance of this is 'Separate Ways', a case of a husband's quietude beyond desperation as observed by his sister-in-law. Both mood and fishing-hotel setting are agreeably reminiscent of Elizabeth Bowen.

In *Secrets* (1977) Bernard McLaverty from Belfast can handle schoolboy superstition-cum-piety with admirable lightness, as in 'The Miraculous Candidate' and grimmer, sadder, piety as in 'Saint Paul could Hit the Nail on the Head'. Both these stories are as pertinent to South as North. They are a far cry from his 'Secrets' which has a theme that might have been treated by Elizabeth Bowen: the discovery by a youth of his great-aunt's love letters. There is an even greater delicacy in 'Anodyne' a story told with so much understatement that one might fancy nothing at all had happened. Yet it probes beautifully the taxing issue of how far Literature affects Life, how far, for instance, a diet of Hopkins and Hemingway can influence behaviour, as distinct from slow ruminative writers like Lancelot Andrewes and Sir Thomas Browne.

The childhood, domestic, and matrimonial stories of Kate Cruise O'Brien from Dublin, *A Gift Horse* (1978), have a dry matter-of-factness and an acidulous humour owing something perhaps to Ivy Compton-Burnett. In 'Trespasses', for instance we learn of a lackadaisical young wife that 'she had a most peculiar and energetic attachment to the kitchen floor. . .'[10] Another distinguished English writer, Angus Wilson, comes to mind both in the dialogue and reflections of 'Some Rain Must Fall'. A young wife 'is possessed of a middle-class conviction that pillaging the state was positively virtuous.'[11] This story about the clashes between the values of two different kinds of middle-class is set in Sheffield but argues for Miss O'Brien as a potential recorder of Dublin's social gradations. She is also very good on aspects of Irish university life (Trinity College, this time) as in 'Henry Died' which in a stunning closing line lights up vistas of vestigial Christianity.

In *The Diamonds at the Bottom of the Sea* (1979) Desmond Hogan from County Galway exposed a vision and a style which more than in any of his contemporaries may be called impressionistic. And while many of his settings are Irish, rural or urban, they are as likely to be in New York or San Francisco, Paris or Rome. More so even than Higgins, he may be called an internationalist, although not infrequently the invocation of foreign places seems arbitrary, if not haphazard. Reading Hogan is like seeing the world by fireworks subsiding into *chiaroscuro*. Like Higgins, he may owe something to Barnes, and perhaps Carson McCullers. He is attracted to significant grotesque and chameleon sexual situations, as may be seen in, for instance, 'A Poet and an Englishman' and from a second collection *The Children of Lir* (1981), in the mythopoeic title story, set in Rome and Dublin's Liberties.

I would note in 1980 four collections by women: *The Lady with the Red Shoes* by Ita Daly from Leitrim; *Female Forms* by Emma Cooke from Laois; *A Season for Mothers* by Helen Lucy Burke from Galway; and *Captives* by F.D. Sheridan from Dublin. Interestingly the four women have, between them, stories set in France, Italy, Spain and Greece. Ita Daly's title story is about a honeymoon in Rome, but it is not her best, given her baulking at a subterranean incest theme. Yet she handles sapphic themes with discreet candour in 'Compassion' and 'Such Good Friends'. In all, she has the virtue of being calmly outrageous. Helen Lucy Burke's Roman story draws a sad, frightening, droll picture of Mother Ireland in the shape of a visiting matron, an immensely pious, chauvinist, bigoted, and immensely funny (if she were not the shape of things that were and are) old person. In 'The Greek Experience' an Irish couple on holiday on a Greek island learn about conscienceless fornication, the husband with an American nymphomaniac, the wife with a Greek student. It is a knowing, brutally frank, and comic tale.

In 'The Greek Trip' Emma Cooke further extends the impression that sexual sophistication is the norm rather than the exception in Irish women writers. That includes deviant sexuality. But there is nothing of that in the Turgenev-esque 'Summer School' (the Merriman School, perhaps?) in which Ms Cooke artfully avoids mush in an exquisite dying fall.

Italy and Ireland, but chiefly Spain, figure in F. D. Sheridan's stories, ten of them in the latter country. Her Spain is not exotic nor even particularly picturesque. Ms Sheridan is writing about the Spain of Franco and her heroines are very much aware of the bitterness surviving from the Civil War, of uncauterised spiritual wounds and timid aspirations. There are indications she may yet be the writer to recreate the Spain of the late fifties and early sixties as seen by Irish eyes that do not always smile. Of her two Irish stories, 'When the Saints Come Tumbling Down' effects a palpable overthrow of appearance, when a woman, disliked if not detested in life, turns out to have been, possibly, a martyr to her family.

Internationalism with a vengeance comes with Niall Quinn from Dublin, in his *Voyavic* (1980) possibly the most exciting book of stories by an Irishman since Higgins's *Felo de Se*. It is fitting that the internationalism should manifest itself initially in the title story in a Hamburg Guest (i.e. immigrant) Workers' Hostel, where Yugoslavs and Turks and Spaniards and ex-French colonials and Irish mingle together: a melting pot for the damnable and the damned. This opening story has a climax in Voyavic's death and its aftermath, 'of a Jacobean horror and loveliness' as I wrote when the book first appeared. Only one of the seven long stories is set in Dublin. 'All is Nothing' handles magistrally the theme of the outsider from the cradle who in mid-adolescence learns the tricks of seeming 'normal': 'But in sleep he would dream. Dream, in the protection of adulthood, the dreams children know, before they lose their minds to sanity.'[12] Quinn might have been writing both of Charlotte's Rochester and Emily's Heathcliffe in the Brontë canon.

Eithne Strong from County Limerick rings further changes in *Patterns* (1981), on domestic and matrimonial complexities. She is primarily, I believe, a radical spirit, but keenly aware of the human values that have survived, however clouded or distorted, in the regimen of bourgeois conservatism. 'Contrasts' and 'Mistress of the Junket' sketch tenderly, never lopsidedly, the tensions wrought in marriage by communication with extramural influences. The stories tell us beautifully that change is as good as unrest. Ms Strong is a poet. Her story 'Spectrum' is almost a prose poem, on the unlikely subject of Dalkey Anglo-Irish dodos.

I must put a stop to this gallop through the Irish short story over the last forty years with a reference to a recent off-beat collection, *Banished Misfortune* (1982) by Dermot Healy from Westmeath/Cavan. Four years older than Desmond Hogan and Neil Jordan, but slower to publish, he shares with them an aversion to formal prose, which often makes, in this reader's case, for sequential confusion. But if Healy has not yet mastered his style, his slanting vision takes in the most complicated relationships among very ordinary people: in the spectral 'Kelly' about Irish in London, with a dimension of Polish agony in exile, in 'The Tenant' about a bank cashier drawn into the petty familial warfare of a country town.

Forty-odd years of the Irish short story, surveyed with inevitable omissions and scant treatments suggest that the tradition consolidated by O'Flaherty, O'Faolain and O'Connor has been modified considerably; that Irish writers are now much more inclined to look at the human condition as distinct from a specifically Irish Catholic condition; above all; that they are bent on exorcising the shades of violent centaurs, first confessions, lovable matriarchs and drunken daddies. The tone, after the times, is predominantly urban. The subjects, in an age of foreign travel for so many, of electronics and ecumenism, of television and contraception, of the spirit of pluralism fighting an uneven battle with the spirit of the Catholic version of puritanism, are increasingly less insular, less self-regarding, more and more cognisant of the doom of man.

13. The Realist Novel after the Second World War

Seán McMahon

There is a sense in which 1945, an appropriate enough line of demarcation for the rest of Europe, has less significance for Ireland. Neutrality which effected its own internal traumas had protected the country from the sense of trial by ordeal and consequently from the sense that things were never going to be the same again. Only the North had been officially at war but since there was no conscription war's full effect was muted and seen in its full savagery only in the Belfast air-raids. Ireland's point of no return was not as precisely stable as any simple date but was a gradual process, admittedly with increasing acceleration, that occurred in the early sixties and one whose forces were increasing affluence, the coming and spread of television, the often disturbing reappraisal of traditional values occasioned by the Second Vatican Council, and, relevant to the writer's position, the paperback revolution. Once the distributors, those modern patrons of literature, had covered the country from Ballycastle to Ballydehob with wire cages filled with books Ireland could no longer remain a protected or, not to break a tooth on the word, a censored country. Enough has been written and said about the Censorship Board to render any further discussion superfluous. It was an institution necessary to the moral self-esteem of the new estate as it struggled for identity and it went in time. Its effects on Irish writers is literally incalculable. Some were not bothered by it, some were publicly exposed, some helped indirectly to break it, and nowadays writers find it hard to imagine such an unlikely institution. Of the first group Francis MacManus and Michael McLaverty continued to write unselfconsiously the books that interested them. MacManus's best book, the only one published outside Ireland, *Fire in the Dust* (1950) continued his chronicle of a

quieter Ireland than the one which particularly from Liam
O'Flaherty and Peadar O'Donnell charted a dramatic, peasant,
edge-of-poverty existence. This rich but narrow vein was
worked right up to the sixties and became such a tradition
that it was reckoned as the mark of the true Irish writer
especially to the not-unsympathetic eye of critics in Britain
and America. As late as 1966 Irving Wardle could write in
The Observer (1.5.66), 'From Brinsley MacNamara to Aidan
Higgins the Irish provincial novel records a low, creeping
existence – solitary figures hoeing sodden fields, island
fishermen deserted by their mackerel shoals.'[1] Benedict Kiely
thinking along the same lines had one of the characters in *The
Captain with the Whiskers* (1960) opine, 'Irish novels are all
mud and misery, all bejasus, all parish priests, all girls having
babies.'[2] MacManus rejected this one-sidedness and causes his
character, John Lee, the diffident schoolteacher hero of *Flow
On Lovely River* to consider the stereotype, as he gazes upon
the rich comfort of the Lennon farmhouse: 'Why don't
Irishmen forsake the eternal bogs and bleak mountain roads
for a while – all part of a small, narrow, and even romantic
view of Ireland – for something like this in which a Dutchman
of the interiors and the tiled floors and the fat burghers would
have delighted with all his soul and every drop of his warm
creative blood.'[3]

MacManus's own work did much to redress the imbalance
and in that last novel blazed the trail of a bourgeois novel and
a critique of small town intolerance. It was ironical that what
Benedict Kiely did differently in *In a Harbour Green* (1949),
The Cards of the Gambler (1952), *Honey Seems Bitter* (1952) and
The Captain with the Whiskers, simply because of a decision
about stage properties and a different humour of writing
should have come in for the dire attentions of the Censorship
Board which in MacManus's own words in a Thomas Davis
Lecture in 1962, 'could ban with a savagery that seems
pathological.'[4] Another writer of the period whose view of
the country was loving but critical, a proper attitude for a
writer it seems to me, was Mervyn Wall. In two suave and
deadly novels, *Leaves for the Burning* (1952) and *No Trophies
Raise* (1956) he rated the by-now self-satisfied new country
for quasi-religious combinations (in the purely legal sense),

for 'Where-were-you-in-1916?' opportunism and for a kind
of aggressive philistinism, and paid the price. When these
books were written the censorship system was at its greatest
strength for like some baleful witch's candle it flamed fiercest
before it died. These writers wrote with an implicit moral
purpose, to deliver the Ireland they perceived to the serious
reader. Yet they had to suffer the obloquy of being, perhaps,
in Brendan Behan's words, 'the best banned in the land' but
still banned. By contrast Michael McLaverty continued to
compose his lovely spare chronicles of dutiful people and their
struggle for life and homestead – books that might have
seemed sentimental had they not dealt with people like the
author, quietly certain about the meaning of their lives and
sustained by a deep, strong faith.

By the time Wardle made his ill-adjudged remarks (in a
review of Richard Power's novel of Aran, *The Land of Youth*)
the literary scene in Ireland had come out of the bogs and
ashore from literary islands. The same semester that saw
Power's book also produced the vastly different *Lucifer Falling*
by Terence de Vere White, *Caliban's Wooing* by Victor Price
and *Langrishe Go Down* by Aidan Higgins which *pace* Wardle
was set far from island or sodden field.

Meanwhile the partitioned North with its loyalist majority
struggled to maintain its anomalous existence. Any writer
who contemplated that society had to face the institutionalised
inequalities and the constant fact of sectarianism kept
permanently plumping for the benefit of a few. It is simplistic
to speak of *nationalist* writers but those who wished to write
realistic novels about the society they lived in had however
implicity to take up a quasi-political stance in their writings.
The Northern Protestant community for this reason did not
produce many novelists and those it did manage to breed found
that they had to reject at least aesthetically the separatism of
the Six Counties. Even the seeking of safety in novels so rural
as to be almost pastoral proved vain as even such apolitical
novelists as Shan Bullock and Anne Crone discovered. One
of the best novelists of the post-war period got round the
problem by writing what are in essence historical novels even
though the existence of two intermittently warring tribes is
not ignored. This is Sam Hanna Bell whose first novel,

December Bride, was published in 1951. It is an account of a Presbyterian *menage-à-trois* on a Strangford Lough farm (rather an unlikely contrivance in the circumstances but based upon an actual case). His description of life on the Echlin farm in a region where papists are few and properly behaved and where the brothers Andrew and Hamilton share the bed of Sarah Gomartin is masterly. The picture of the country year, the detail of the farm work and the reaction of a society as straitlaced and for the same kind of reasons as Moses's Israelites is unique in that it came from inside, so to speak, told by an artist whose instincts are consonant with the society while his stance is that of the detached observer. *The Hollow Ball* followed ten years later and provides us with a unique account of a city which regularly in the news for the last hundred years has rarely been written about by the clinically benevolent novelist. The story of David Minnis, the counter-jumper who became a professional footballer, recreates the thirties commercial life of The Black City to use the title of an unjustly neglected novel of Belfast life by Malachy Caulfield. It serves as a reminder that economic deprivation produced the expected viciousness of the extremes on both sides and that the left-wing intellectual conscience was as active and probably as ineffectual in Belfast as in other cities at the time. Bell's third novel, *A Man Flourishing* (1974) is an account of the establishment of the nucleus of what was to become the Victorian industrial city and of the eclipse of the nonconformist republican tradition of the United Irishmen.

Also associated with Strangford Lough, that lesion in the body of County Down, is Joseph Tomelty who was born in Portaferry at the mouth of the lough. Famous as a writer of plays both light and dark he also wrote two novels, just reissued, *Red is the Port Light* (1948) a dark tale of coastal shipping, bastardy and madness, and *The Apprentice* (1953) subtitled 'The Story of a Nonentity' based upon his own experiences in the decorating trade, which gives another valuable look at the working-class life of the city.

Maurice Leitch, author of four novels about Ulster, is another significant Northern novelist and like Bell a useful one in that he can write critically about the Northern majority from the inside. His first novel, *The Liberty Lad* (1965) was a vigorous young man's impatient look at the accursed province. Frank Glass, a teacher full of sixties confidence and mixed sexual drive is notably critical of his father's mill-owning employers and the way they exploit the loyalty (in every sense) of their workers. He also limns the basic savagery of Orangeism however inactive in peacetime. *Stamping Ground* (1975) tells of the adolescence of the same Frank Glass spent in a very unpermissive society with sectarianism a distant threat like summer thunder. *Poor Lazarus* (1969) and *Silver's City* (1981) came closer to the raw violence of the North. The first published just at the start of the Troubles turns a prophetic eye upon the harsher aspects of the Protestant community while the second actually penetrates the dark city which his earlier novels used circle so warily. Now the imposthumes have burst making night hideous. Silver Steel is a Protestant terrorist folk-hero who has compromised his extremism in prison and therefore must be eliminated. His fight for survival in what has become an alien city is reminiscent of *Odd Man Out* (1945), F. L. Green's novel of the IRA. In neither is the actual organisation described nor its motives discussed. Leitch's attempt to make sense of the Northern situation is oddly moving and it gives to his book an extra pathos.

Anthony C. West though twenty years older than Leitch also faced up to sectarianism in his novels, *The Ferret Fancier* (1963) and *As Towns with Fire* (1968) but his heroes Simon Green and Christopher MacMannan are too gloriously self-obsessed with their own growth and that of the teeming land in which they live to let that bitterness hurt. The first of these is a remarkable unblinking account of an Ulster adolescence; the second is longer and perhaps less controlled, but its Irish sections are illuminating especially the account of life in Belfast during the Blitz. Consideration of Belfast in wartime inevitably calls to mind Brian Moore, an author of prodigious talent and the Irish novelist of the period who is most highly regarded in England and America. *Judith Hearne* (1955), *The Feast of Lupercal* (1958), *The Emperor of Ice-Cream* (1966), *The Doctor's Wife* (1976) and *The Temptation of Eileen Hughes* (1980) are set in his native city. It would be impossible to write about the city without some note of its disease but Moore with characteristic irony takes an oblique view. Diarmuid Devine, the feckless Catholic teacher of *The Feast of Lupercal* muses, 'Protestant girls are fast', and the Shankill Road Blitz victim in *The Emperor of Ice-Cream* will not risk the ministrations of nuns in a Fenian hospital like the Mater: 'Take me to the Royal Victoria   boys!' In more than a dozen novels Moore covers many aspects of what we may call Irish life: the pressures of religion, the guilt and over-the-shoulder-look of the successful Irish exile and the strange capers that true lovers run into. The technical brilliance of the writing flavoured here and there with transatlantic expressions (Moore had lived out of the country for nearly forty years) and the confidence which enables him to handle fantasy, gothic horror, social realism and sexuality, especially of women, make him a dauntingly impressive writer. He seems fascinated by religious belief as *Judith Hearne, Catholics* (1972) and his most recent novel, *Cold Heaven* (1983) indicate, while retaining a detached, agnostic position. This detachment has caused at least one critic, Professor John Cronin of Queen's, to wish for 'a thawing of the ice about his heart.'[5] In spite of this coldness he remains one of our very finest writers.

Finally before we leave the North mention should be made of two 'sports' in the biological sense of failing to fall within reasonable catagories. The first, Jack Wilson wrote three novels in the sixties, *The Wild Summer* (1963), *The Tomorrow Country* (1968) and *Dark Eden* (1969), all of which are mixtures of Presbyterianism and country lust. The last of the three is set in the period of the Ulster Plantations but it is too concerned with personal passion and individual greed to offer any insights. More is confidently expected from Sam Hanna Bell's novel-in-progress, *Across the Narrow Seas,* which will be more historically realised. The other is Ian Cochrane who self-exiled from his native mid-Antrim since 1949 writes with horribly effective detail of poor lower-than-working-class Protestant enclaves where violence and madness are commonplace, as the titles of his novels, *A Streak of Madness* (1972) and *Gone in the Head* (1974) underscore. Neither of these writers is mainstream but Cochrane because of his unusual view of a traditionally correct and upright people and his distinct if alarming professional voice is a writer of some significance.

If this were a longer survey, a critical volume rather than a shortish essay, then one chapter at least should be given to what we might warily call the Anglo-Irish tradition. We might even be bolder and call it the Southern Protestant tradition except that Caroline Blackwood's sharp County Down voice might remind us that the Border is patently artificial in that respect too. It is worth remembering that the great Anglo-Irish centaur, Edith Somerville, did not die until 1949. When she and her more talented companion were not being funny about horses their tendency was towards the gothic and with the prophetic sensibility of your true writer could predict change and decay in all around they saw. A clear line runs from them through Elizabeth Bowen and Helen Wykham to the funniest latterday exponent, Mollie Keane with *Good Behaviour* (1982) and *Time After Time* (1983), who delineates with wicked accuracy this rich decay. One writer who looks at the Anglo-Irish with sympathy and humour but without relish at its crumbling is Jennifer Johnston. Five out of six of her novels deal with the meeting, the clash and finally the mesh of the two traditions. Customary, almost compulsory, elements of black comedy and wilfulness are absent from her work which is still funny in spite of an inevitable, concomitant poignancy. Indeed all but the most resolutely radical must feel some sense of pathos at the passing of a way of life however privileged or even rapacious. Certainly the novels about it have a great strength and individual flavour. *Langrishe, Go Down* of all Aidan Higgins's books for this reason remains clearest in the memory. Samuel Beckett's novels may as well be mentioned here as anywhere. *Murphy* (1938), *Watt* (1944) and *Molloy* (1951) might with violence be fitted into an Anglo-Irish category but with *Malone Dies* (1956) we are in familiar Beckettian surroundings, a bare inescapable room, the only Irish element left the gift of the gab but not any longer capable of meaning. One could claim to find Beckettian elements in Flann O'Brien too but the garrulousness of *The Hard Life* (1961), *The Dalkey Archive* (1964), and *The Third Policeman* (1967), is at least entertaining and in touch with *some* reality. O'Brien is cultish and a vigorously defended national treasure which is beyond criticism. The literary historian may merely note that the world is a male one, a middle-aged one and an asexual one, and one in which the place of women is enough to cause even the mildest feminist to choke with spleen.

Two Whites, Terence de Vere and Jack present yet another view of our mixed society. Jack White's *One For the Road* (1956) gives a remarkably interesting picture of wartime Dublin and the psychological effect of neutrality; *The Hard Man* (1958) joyously contrasted Protestant and Catholic *mores;* and *The Devil You Know* (1962) gives the best picture of modern artistic and academic Dublin in its brief prime of self-confidence and affluence. Terence in a series of even more urbane books, *Lucifer Falling* (1966), *Tara* (1967), *The Lambert Mile* (1969) and *The March Hare* (1970) chronicled what now seems if not a golden age at least a pinchbeck one. Yet even here in his 1973 novel, *The Distance and the Dark* the shadow and actual brutishness of the Northern troubles irrupt. This recurring topic of violence brings me to a novel of great worth and significance which though set a hundred years before the present neatly combines consideration of the gentry, the clergy and the infective nature of community violence. I refer to *The Big Chapel* (1971) by Thomas Kilroy which when it was published was a neat analogue to the recrudescent equivalent brutality in the North. It also contained in Fr Lannigan a priest-portrait equalled only by Francis MacManus with Fr James in *The Greatest of These* and by Richard Power's Fr Conroy in The Hungry Grass (1969).

I am certain that John Broderick would not for one moment accept the Irving Wardle description of a low creeping existence. He has found the Midlands of Ireland and in particular the town of Athlone a place as susceptible to literary rendering as Wessex or Yoknapatawpha County. In a series of novels in particular, *The Pilgrimage* (1961), *The Fugitives* (1962), *The Waking of Willie Ryan* (1965) and *An Apology for Roses* (1973), he has added a new dimension, a look at the subtext of the cosy Irish town, wickeder perhaps but no longer as stifling as Kiely found Omagh in *Land Without Stars* (1946) and *In a Harbour Green*.

I have mentioned the Censorship Board (indeed how could I avoid it?) and I am convinced it disappeared when it did because of society's change. Yet two writers at least hastened its departure catalytically rather than deliberately. (I hope that as a devout non-scientist I've got that right!) These were Edna O'Brien and John McGahern. They dealt frankly but by no means lickerishly with sexual matters and they drew down the automatic, and it still seems mindless disapproval of the Board. McGahern had a kind of revenge with his latest novel, *The Pornographer* (1979) which showed how dire and inert that kind of writing was and implied that a salutary control that society probably needs was dissipated in unco-guidness and bloody-mindedness. Edna O'Brien's almost hypnotic voice caused a sensation with her first two books as her *Country Girls* Kate and Baba grew and were shaped in the thickets of small town prejudice. Her later books develop the theme of the vulnerable women in a world of heedless and basically untrustworthy men. None of these has the surefootedness as when she is writing about home. Her account of the lives of the schoolgirls and later the young women of the forties and fifties at home in County Clare and loosed in Dublin is quite authentic. Even the hesitancies and reticences of the writing are true to the period. McGahern's view of life is darker and in spite of the writing's control more intense. *The Barracks* (1963) brought a new unromantic realism to the portrayal of Irish life and the description of the death from cancer of the stepmother Mrs Regan is justly famous. The book is, I think, a finer piece of work than its more notorious successor, *The Dark* (1965) with its detail of adolescent masturbation and its characterisation of a homosexual priest. *The Leavetaking* (1974) has the same sense of autobiographical origin and its account of the love affair and marriage of Patrick and Isobel and of their Joycean hegira is memorable.

Finally room must be made for two further writers of undoubted stature: Julia O'Faolain and John Banville. The first, deserving the quasi-Celtic description of 'famous daughter of famous father' is like him a marvellous writer of short stories but in the withdrawn *Godded and Codded* (1970), an account of an Irish Candida abroad in Paris, *Women in the Wall* (1975) her dazzling novel of monastery life in Merovingian Gaul, *No Country for Young Men* (1980) a bitterly ironic look at the Irish freedom-fighting delirium, and *The Obedient Wife* (1982) which turns feminism on its head and back again, she shows a powerful mixture of cerebral and emotional writing, sensual music with unageing intellect spun into one. Her women, for she is really a feminist if with a small 'f', seem not only biologically but in every other way more perfectly evolved than men yet they continue to let themselves be trapped by these same men driven by some incandescent urge. John Banville beginning with two fresh and quite brilliant novels, *Long Lankin* (1970) and *Birchwood* (1973), (I am not so sure about *Nightspawn* [1971]), has had an astronomical output since, if I may be allowed the stellar pun. *Dr Copernicus* (1976) and *Kepler* (1981) are far from fictionalised biographies and with *The Newtown Letter* (1982) while keeping one finger in his planetary pie he has placed himself once again in the forefront of contemporary novelists.

The passing of the temporary period of affluence has done nothing to stem the flow of new novels and recent years have seen a great resurgence in Irish publishing. Emma Cooke, Maura Treacy, Neil Jordan, Desmond Hogan, Bernard McLaverty, Patrick McGinley, Leland Bardwell have all written impressive novels and most were published at home. Though it is too early yet to be sure about the exact nature of this renaissance the prospects are pleasing. Irish writers still seem to find it less daunting to write stories over intervals until they have enough assembled to make a book and as far as native product is concerned collections of stories have outnumbered novels. However the Wardle stereotype has long ago been blasted to scorn. Ireland, the troubled country, no longer enjoying the advantages and disadvantages of a relatively isolated existence still provides her writers with material. The time may have at last come when Sean O'Faolain's forties crack no longer applies. For better or worse Ireland has ceased to be the country where 'God smiles, the priest beams and the novelist groans.'[6]

14. Literary Biography in Twentieth–Century Ireland

Maurice Harmon

The publication of a number of important literary biographies in recent years has focused attention on this paricular form of writing. These include the revised edition of Richard Ellmann's *James Joyce* (1982), which combines factual biographical detail with literary criticism. Although it has been criticised for some factual errors and for its tendency to accept oral evidence too readily, it is nevertheless a major and influential literary biography. Biographies since Ellmann's have tended to be written with a similar all–inclusive use of detail, as though he had set a standard that all must follow. Some of these have also been explicit about their subject's failings. Ian Hamilton's *Robert Lowell* (1983), for example, is both massive in its documentation in the Ellmann manner and frank about Lowell's mental disturbances. Humphrey Carpenter's *W. H. Auden* (1981) is similarly weighty in factual detail and open about his homosexuality.

For some reason Irish writers have not attracted native biographers as much as one might have expected. It may be that the Irish prefer to talk about their writers than to write about them. Then again the intimate nature of Irish society may inhibit the biographer. In a small country it is difficult to write fully and objectively about someone whose family, relatives and friends are still living. In addition biography in some quarters is regarded as a gentlemanly activity, not the kind of thing that serious critics and scholars should indulge in. This view, however, can hardly be sustained in the face of the kind of work done by Ellmann, Hamilton and Carpenter. There is nevertheless a lingering notion that biography ought to remain free of the rigours and excesses of modern critical writing.

When we look more closely at our subject, which is

biographies by Irish writers and biographies of Irish writers written by other Irish writers, we find that there are two outstanding biographers: Joseph Hone and Sean O'Faolain.

Joseph Hone wrote two biographies: *The Life of George Moore* (1936) and *W. B. Yeats 1865-1939* (1943, and revised in 1967 after Hone's death). The two biographies are interesting for their contrasting methods and because they are unequal in merit. In the case of Moore, Hone's task was made easier because he was dealing with a writer who had written books and essays about himself. In addition there was a generous supply of letters from Moore himself and from his relations and friends. Several people had even written their reminiscences about him. It may be, however, that this abundance of source material made it difficult for Hone to shape the biography, to discover and to clarify his own portrait of a subject that already existed in some complexity. Moore seems to have been fascinated and puzzled by himself. He reflected upon himself in several memoirs, but autobiography is an imprecise measure of a man's true nature. Therefore, for the biographer the existence of autobiographical work by the subject he is trying to describe can be both a support and a barrier. It provides evidence that is both challenging and suspect. Already an autobiographical portrait, or portraits, exist and that makes the biographer's task more difficult.

Moore emerges in Hone's biography as a changeable, impulsive, sensitive man who seems to have been insecure in most relationships and to have had difficulty in knowing the effect he had on others. There are many fascinating periods in his life, such as the long artistic apprenticeship in France, and the somewhat comic period in Ely Place. And there are several interesting elements, such as his fussy interference in his brother's family and his enigmatic relationships with women. Above all there is the story of his gradual emergence as an important writer and his dedication to his work. Hone knows the work, summarises it and occasionally offers some criticism, but literary evaluation is not his main intention.

Despite the richness and variety of the subject, Hone's biography is disappointing. This is partly the result of bad organisation. The book is marred by a confusing use of detail and by an inadequate shaping of material. It is as though

THE GENIUS OF IRISH PROSE

Hone's purpose was to collect and present the components of a biography from which the reader is to select at will elements to create his own portrait. The organisation of material in individual chapters is loose and there is a general lack of coherence. Another failing, giving the work an amateurish air, is the absence of proper footnotes. This makes it impossible at times to separate the biographer's views from those of his subject and one cannot verify his use of evidence. He also uses secondary sources, such as letters, in an uncritical manner. A further difficulty arises from his tendency not to identify living people, although it is difficult to discover what ground-rules he is following. Thus he does not name the Monsignor who wrote 'anonymously in an Irish newspaper'[1] attacking the theology of *The Countess Cathleen,* but at the same time he disposes of Yeats's claim that it was a monk and of Moore's claim that it was a friar! Similarly, he identifies the 'Stella' of *Hail and Farewell* as Clara Christian but does not identify her female companion. He also mentions what he calls Moore's 'outrageous' attack on Mahaffy and tells us that it appeared in 'a saucy journal of Nationalist and Catholic opinion',[2] but he does not identify the journal!

Finally, the biography is weak on psychology. Too much is unexamined, as for example, Moore's relationship with his mother. Hone quotes liberally from their correspondence but without investigating it. He is equally lax in the case of Moore's relationships with women. He seems to have had an almost endless succession of love affairs, some actual, some fantasy, but Hone makes no attempt to understand them or to measure the degree of Moore's involvement.

Hone's life of Yeats, however, is more satisfying. There is less reliance on quotations from letters and more attention given to specifying sources and to separating Hone's own views from those of Yeats. The more compact organisation makes it helpful and informative in its outline of Yeats's career in which Hone identifies successive events and people who influenced it. He creates a complex portrait that provides the social and political contexts for the writing. One has a sense of the external life – the conflicts with others, the discussions, the relationships with Lady Gregory, Maud Gonne, George Moore, his father, the involvement with the theatre, the occult, politics and these are all part of the contexts within which he wrote. This method is particularly helpful in the early period when there was a striking gap between the lyrics of *The Wind among the Reeds* (1899), for example, and what Yeats was actually doing at the time. From the outset one feels that Hone's critical sense of Yeats is more confident than it was in the case of Moore. The critical observations may not be profound but they are sensible. Thus of *The Wind among the Reeds* he wrote: 'That he had advanced in technical accomplishment admitted of no doubt. There was far less of unnecessary beauty than in the earlier volume; he was no longer carried away by every fancy into the side images which marred the directness of the "Rose" poems. The more characteristic, the dimmer and more esoteric poems in *The Wind among the Reeds* – those which bear the signature of what he afterwards called a dream-burdened will – create a curious effect of isolation in the whole body of the work; and it is significant that of all his books this was the one which he revised least for republication. These lyrics must be pre-Raphaelite or nothing.'[3]

One reason for the improved quality of the Yeats biography is that Yeats is seen as a more serious figure. He pursues experience with a palpable intensity so that the object becomes more important than himself. Drawn as we are with him in pursuit of new ideas or fresh experience we do not pause to reflect upon the man. Significantly, Hone's biography has yet to be surpassed. Some incidents have been enlarged upon by later writers as more evidence has come to light. Hone's account of Margot Ruddock, for example, has been expanded by Roger McHugh in *Ah, Sweet Dancer* (1970) and George Harper has greatly increased our understanding of Yeats and the occult. Many topics have been enriched by more concentrated study. Nevertheless, Hone's biography is very good – intelligent, perceptive, balanced and written with clarity and verve.

It is also a humanising book. Yeats the man who seems to disappear within the quest for wisdom finally gains a numinous and attractive aura. There is, for example, Yeats the lecturer in America, being deliberately oratorical. In a letter to Lady Gregory he explains: 'I am working at this speech as

I never worked at a speech before. . . I have already dictated the whole speech once; indeed, I have already dictated some parts of it several times, and I am now going to go through it all again. Then I shall go down to the hall and speak the whole lecture in the empty space. This is necessary, because I have found out that the larger the audience the more formal, rhythmical, oratorical must one's delivery be.'[4] At Notre Dame, where he is at this point on the tour, he gave four lectures in one day and then sat up late telling ghost stories with the priests! Another humanising detail is his sympathy for Maud Gonne during the period of her divorce and the fact that he always showed courtesy and kindness to her friends. Finally there is his sharing of an amusing incident in a letter to Olivia Shakespeare. It was about a visiting actress at the Abbey Theatre and the stage manager who reported about her behaviour to Yeats as follows: '. . . I went to Miss ——'s room. I knocked and she said, "Who is there?" I said, "Stage Manager." She said, "Come in." I went in and there she was, saving your presence, bollicky naked. I turned my head away and there she was facing me in the mirror. I went out and she said, "What do you want?" I said, ·"The crown," and she gave it to me, stretching out her long bare arm. I don't mind seeing a comedian in her knickers but nothing like this was ever seen in the Abbey before. At first I was not going to tell you – I did not want to insult your mind with such a story. They do that kind of thing in England but not here.'[5]

Sean O'Faolain has written several biographies: *The Life Story of Eamon de Valera* (1932), *Constance Markievicz, or The Average Revolutionary* (1934), *King of the Beggars, A Life of Daniel O'Connell, the Irish Liberator in a Study of the Rise of the Modern Irish Democracy (1775-1847)* (1938), *De Valera* (1939), *The Great O'Neill, a Biography of Hugh O'Neill, Earl of Tyrone, 1550-1616* (1942), and *Newman's Way, the Odyssey of John Henry Newman* (1952). Of these the most important are the lives of Daniel O'Connell and Hugh O'Neill.

King of the Beggars is a psychological study written with intellectual vigour, examining, questioning, arguing for particular interpretations and capable of a large compassion and understanding. It is a warts–and–all portrait that is guided by the conviction that it is wrong to idealise O'Connell and foolish not to admit his unattractive qualities, such as his guile and pretence. O'Faolain's fascination with the complexity of O'Connell which he pursues with zest and tact makes the biography exciting to read. We are drawn into the mystery of O'Connell; its components are skilfully analysed, the conclusions are honestly laid before us, making us think about them, weighing the evidence that has been provided, reflecting on the arguments.

O'Faolain's book is interesting in a variety of ways, not least of which is his relish for argument. He loves to probe and analyse and speculate. He admires mental ingenuity. He also paints a realistic portrait of the man – his reactions to the 1798 rebellion, his disgust with his own sluggishness, his driving ambition, his broad humour, his loneliness, his boldness. It is a psychological *tour de force*. And it has its miserable background in the dregs of the eighteenth and early nineteenth-century Ireland. The growling of the dispossessed are much clearer to O'Faolain's ear than the colourful antics of the Ascendancy boozers and duellists.

But it is not an objective biography. O'Faolain sees O'Connell as a model for his own time. He emphasises two qualities in particular: his lack of sectarianism and his definition of the relationship of church and state. Historical biography becomes a kind of exemplum, a drama of achievement and of ideals of behaviour by which twentieth-century Irish democracy may be guided. Thus O'Faolain quotes O'Connell's opposition to the Act of Union. 'I know,' O'Connell said, 'that the Catholics of Ireland still remember they have a country, and that they would never accept any advantages as a sect that would destroy them as a people.' O'Faolain comments on that with enthusiasm: 'There is vision behind that declaration. It is so fine, so early, so bold, generous, and statesmanlike. It cut across sectarianism to nationality. It was the kind of thing Tone and the United Irishmen had sought for far and wide, and found nowhere except among enlightened Protestants. Here was a man of the people accepting the oneness of Ireland, inside the historical fact of conquest and invasion, because to his realistic and pragmatical mind the mingled strain in Irish life was something that, accepted, could create a new nation. It was the appeal of the first national leader, since the fall of the Gaelic State, to the remnants of its fall, to build Freedom on Conquest.'[6]

O'Connell's definition of the relationship that should exist between church and state is also stressed. It is seen in his reaction to Grattan's Relief Bill of 1813 which had an oath of allegiance that all Catholics would be asked to take. O'Connell denounced the idea of suborning the clergy. 'Does any man,' he asked, 'imagine that this Catholic religion will prosper in Ireland if our prelates, instead of being what they are at present, shall become the tools of the administration? They would lose all respect for themselves, all respectability in the eyes of others.'[7] A certain amount of simplification results from using history in this polemical way, as part of O'Faolain's own engagement with Irish society and politics in his own time.

Even in the case of Hugh O'Neill, O'Faolain's interests go beyond the objective recording and assessment of historical events and the analysis of human motive and behaviour. Just as O'Connell embodied the needs of his people, so did O'Neill at the end of the sixteenth century. And just as O'Connell expressed the intricacies of the Irish mind, so did O'Neill in his protracted negotiations with the Tudors which were a maze of statement and qualification, seeming peace and secret rebellion. But perhaps what brings the two men closest in O'Faolain's view is their creative capacity. Both lived at a time of social breakdown, when one civilisation was at an end and another needed to be created. O'Connell carried the peasants with him into a modern democracy, O'Neill had the vision to move beyond the fragmented Gaelic civilisation into some sense of a unified country. O'Faolain's contrasting pictures of the old Gaelic system and of the new Tudor system are masterly, showing how great was the ignorance on both sides of what the other stood for. It is to O'Neill's credit, in O'Faolain's view, that he was able to transcend those differences, could see the weaknesses in the Irish system, could parry Tudor aggression, biding his time, and then, when faced with the inevitable advance of invasion into the north, could try to rally the whole country round the potentially unifying idea of the Counter-Reformation. While the portrait of O'Neill lacks the almost super-human variety of the O'Connell portrait, it is nevertheless a fascinating reconstruction and interpretation of a man who was ruthless, intelligent and cunning and who, like O'Connell, tried to bridge the gap between the old and the new, the doomed world of the old pastoral, fragmented Gaelic order and the new, unified, centralised world of the Renaissance. That he went down to defeat at Kinsale gives him a tragic dimension which is not present in O'Connell. 'He was,' in O'Faolain's words, 'the modern man who had tried to bear up the rotting edifice of antiquity, and has fallen under its weight.'[8]

Naturally, because social conditions were so very different in the sixteenth century there is less application of the idea of O'Neill as a model for twentieth-century Irish leaders. But there is the lesson of his ability to introduce creative ideas from outside his own country. In O'Faolain's view, whenever a country runs into a stagnant period in which there is no discernible pattern for the future, one way out of the impasse is to introduce fertile ideas from abroad.

While O'Faolain and Hone are the outstanding biographers, several other Irish biographies have been written. These include Frank O'Connor's *The Big Fellow, A Life of Michael Collins* (1937), Ulick O'Connor's *The Times I've Seen: Oliver St John Gogarty* (1963) and *Brendan Behan* (1970) and Terence de Vere White's three biographies: *The Road of Excess* (1946), *Kevin OHiggins* (1948) and *The Parents of Oscar Wilde, Sir William and Lady Wilde* (1967). All of these are of interest, informative and lively in style but *The Road of Excess* is the most impressive of them, comparable to O'Faolain's life of O'Connell, being full of politics and legal issues. It brings Isaac Butt alive in the context of his time and traces the process by which he replaced O'Connell as leader of the Irish people and was in turn replaced by Parnell. It is not a eulogistic biography. Thus when Butt makes his political stand clear in the following speech, de Vere White comments on the weakness of the position. Butt was speaking in defence of the Act of Union and in opposition to O'Connell's agitation for its repeal. 'I am,' he said, 'quite willing to discuss this question as an Irishman. I am not − I cannot be indifferent to the prosperity of the British Empire − I could not contemplate without dismay the breaking up of that mighty dynasty − the downfall of that noble power. Nay, more, I believe with Pitt that no one can speak as a true Englishman who does not speak as a true Irishman, or as a true Irishman who does not speak as a true Englishman. I am satisfied that we all have a much greater stake in the strength and in the prosperity of the Empire at large, than we can have in any petty and separate interest of any of its component parts.'[9] De Vere White's comment on this is blunt. Irishmen, he writes, who shared Butt's views have always been willing to overlook the interest of their own country at England's call. When, he asks, 'when has an Englishman spoken as a true Irishman? Pitt talked nonsense. With his keen mind and analytical brain it is difficult to understand how Butt could have trotted out Pitt's convenient little phrase without realising its obvious untruth. The fact of the matter is now, as it always has been, that Unionism is an entirely sentimental creed, the love of the colonial for the mother country.'[10]

There is a sense of commitment and of identification with the subject in this biography that is lacking in de Vere White's other biographies. Occasionally, he draws parallels with situations in modern Ireland, but the main emphasis is on the man's political and legal careers. He admires his highly successful defence of the men of 1848 and the men of 1867. He traces his rise to political eminence and his decline and attributes his lack of success in the House of Commons to his inherent respect for the institution and for its members. His argument is persuasive. Butt, he writes, was 'steeped in history and full of the tradition of parliament. . . To him, that institution brought visions of Chatham, Fox, Pitt, Burke and Canning. To Parnell, it was an organisation for the perpetuation of injustice abroad and the accumulation of self-satisfaction at home.'[11] Butt, he argues, overestimated his personal influence in the House. It is significant that his name is hardly mentioned in the lives of Gladstone and Disraeli.

This novelist and biographer enjoys unravelling and assessing the public issues and conflicts, but he also characterises the man. 'One can,' he writes, 'imagine him very well – big and benevolent, ingratiating, full of good talk; eyes, brilliant black, passing from learned discourse to Hiberno-legal anecdote; profound, humorous, pathetic; striking, occasionally, a note embarrassing to those who are apt to conceal their piety, addicted at the same time to whiskey-punch; prepared to play whist all night and appear in court next morning.' But his most vivid portrait of Butt comes almost as an aside in *The Parents of Oscar Wilde*. It comes in an ironical miniature of Butt during his defence of Mary Josephine Travers during her libel action against Lady Wilde that turned out to be a case for alleged rape against Sir William. Butt might well have thought, writes de Vere White, '"There but for the grace of God, go I." Capable of every generous action, noble-hearted and noble-minded, with illegitimate children of his own, on whose desk were placed every day begging or threatening letters, who had distinguished himself in the brothels as well as at the Bar, who kept women from time to time, and could seldom send home more that £1 although his income at the Bar was estimated at £6,000 after his return – he was able to work up virtuous indignation at Wilde's shabby treatment of this vindictive girl. But this gift of sympathy is essential to the successful barrister.'[12]

Biography as a subject requires a more thorough examination than has been possible in this short essay from which we have had to omit hagiography, biographies written by professional historians and many popular lines. There are different kinds of biography: those that entertain and inform us with the factual details of the subject's life; those that analyse and interpret character and behaviour; those that define and assess the forces that influenced the subject in his particular period; and those that aspire to being portraits of an age. The latter combine the characteristics of all the others with a larger perspective that includes the intellectual, political, cultural and social currents of the time; they can only be written of major figures, such as Yeats or Joyce. But all, as Dr J. B. Lyons remarked at the launch of his life of Tom Kettle, all require curiosity and sympathy on the part of the biographer. And it seems, biography becomes a habit. When you write one, you tend to write another.

Notes

1: The Nineteenth Century: A Retrospect

1. Edmund Curtis, *A History of Ireland,* London: Methuen, 1936, p, 355.
2. A. J. C. Hare (ed.), *The Life and Letters of Maria Edgeworth,* London: Edward Arnold, 1894, vol. ii, p. 202.
3. *Edinburgh Review,* February 1826, p. 358.
4. Gerald Griffin, *The Rivals and Tracy's Ambition,* London: E. Bull, 1829, vol. iii, p. 296.
5. Ibid., pp. 297-8.
6. Thomas Flanagan, *The Irish Novelists 1800-1850,* New York: Columbia Univeristy Press, 1959, p. 38.
7. *Athenaeum,* No. 1020 (May 1847), p. 517.
8. W. J. McCormack, *Sheridan Le Fanu and Victorian Ireland,* Oxford: University Press, 1980. See, in particular, chs. 1 and 2.
9. From a letter to Dr Corry quoted in Introduction to *The Life of William Carleton,* London: Downey and Co., 1886, vol. I, p. lv.

2: George Moore and his Irish Novels

1. *Representative Irish Tales.* Compiled with an Introduction and Notes by W. B. Yeats. Edited with a Foreword by Mary Helen Thuente. Gerrards Cross: Colin Smythe Ltd, 1979, p. 25.
2. Susan L. Mitchell. *George Moore.* Dublin: Talbot Press, n.d., p. 43.
3. George Moore. *A Drama in Muslin.* With an Introduction by A. Norman Jeffares. Gerrards Cross: Colin Smythe Ltd, 1981, p. 23. This edition is a reprinting of the seventh edition, published by William Heinemann, London. The novel was originally published by Vizetelly in 1886 after it had appeared in the *Court and Society Review.*
4. Ibid., p. 23.
5. Ibid., p. 153.
6. Ibid., p. 95.
7. See the penultimate diary entry dated 26 April in the final chapter of James Joyce's *A Portrait of the Artist as a Young Man* (1916).
8. George Moore. *The Lake.* Revised edition, 1921. Reprinted with an Afterword by Richard Allen Cave. Gerrards Cross: Colin Smythe Ltd, 1980, p. 129.
9. Ibid., p. 17.
10. Ibid., p. 30.
11. See Richard Allen Cave. 'Turgenev and Moore: *A Sportsman's Sketches* and *The Untilled Field' (The Way Back: George Moore's 'The Untilled Field' and 'The Lake'.* Edited by Robert Welch. Dublin: Wolfhound Press, 1982, pp. 45-63.) where I analyse the emergence of what Moore called his 'dry' style.
12. *The Lake,* p. 102.
13. Ibid., p. 139.
14. Ibid., p. 179.

3: The Short Story: 1900-1945

1. James Joyce, *Dubliners.* Harmondsworth: Penguin Books, 1956, p. 96.

2. Ibid., p. 173.
3. Ibid., p. 104.
4. Manuscript journal in library of University College, Cork.
5. Frank O'Connor, *Day Dreams and other stories*. London: Pan Books, 1973, p. 73.
6. Sean O'Faolain, *Foreign Affairs and other stories*. Harmondsworth: Penguin Books, 1978, p. 9.
7. Frank O'Connor (ed.), *Modern Irish Short Stories*, London: Oxford University Press, 1957, pp. 136f.
8. Mary Lavin, *The Stories of Mary Lavin*. London: Constable, 1964, p. 254.

4: The Realist Novel: 1900-1945
1. Sean O'Faolain, *Vive Moi*. Boston: Little, Brown, 1964, p. 112.
2. James Stephens, *The Charwoman's Daughter*. London: Macmillan, 1912, pp. 115–16.
3. Extract from a letter of Martin Ross to Edith Somerville, dated 8 March 1912.
4. Elizabeth Bowen, *The Last September*. London: Constable, 1929, p. 43.
5. Ibid., p. 44.
6. Sean O'Faolain's remark about 'the alliance between the Church and new businessmen and the politicians, all three nationalist, isolationist. . .' in 'Fifty years of Irish Writing', *Studies,* Spring 1962, p. 97.
7. Patrick Kavanagh, *Tarry Flynn*. Dublin: Mayflower, 1948, p. 20
8. Ibid., p. 21.

5: The Historical Novel
1. George Moore, *A Story-Teller's Holiday*. London: Heinemann, 1928. Vol. II, pp. 100–1.
2. Thomas Flanagan, *The Year of the French*. 1979; reprint: London, Arrow Paperback, 1980, p. 637.
3. Ibid., p. 616.
4. Ibid., p. 617.
5. Ibid., p. 294.
6. *Pacata Hibernia* (Ireland Appeased and Reduced) by Thomas Stafford. London, 1633. Edited and with introduction and notes by Standish O'Grady. London: Downey & Co., 1896. Vol. I, p. 248.
7. Ibid., Vol. I, p. 231, Editor's Note.
8. Ibid., Vol. I, p. 290, Editor's Note.
9. Ibid., Vol. I, p. 138, Editor's Note.
10. J. M. Flood, *The Life of Chevalier Charles Wogan*. Dublin: Talbot Press, 1922.
11. Francis MacManus, *Stand and Give Challenge*. Dublin: Talbot Press, 1934, Foreword.
12. Ibid., pp. 73–4.
13. Ibid., p. 76.
14. Thomas Kilroy, *The Big Chapel*. London: Faber, 1971, p. 137.

6: The Autobiographical Novel
1. James Joyce, *A Portrait of the Artist as a Young Man*. London: Jonathan Cape, 1917, p. 283.
2. Ibid., p. 286.
3. John McGahern, *The Dark*. London: Faber and Faber, 1965, p. 188.
4. Michael McLaverty, *Call My Brother Back*. Dublin: Poolbeg, 1982. p. 183.
5. Ibid., p. 184.
6. Patrick Kavanagh, *Tarry Flynn*. London: Macgibbon and Kee, 1965, p. 173.

7. Ibid., p. 160.
8. As quoted in Swales, *The German Bildungsroman from Wieland to Hesse*. Princeton University Press, p. 159.
9. Michael Farrell, *Thy Tears Might Cease*. London: Hutchinson, 1963, p. 384.
10. Francis Stuart, *Black List: Section H*. Southern Illinois University Press, 1971, p. 45.
11. 'Meet Mr Patrick Kavanagh', *The Bell*, XVI, No. 1, April 1948, p. 7.

7: The Fiction of James Joyce
1. The best text of Joyce's *Portrait of the Artist as a Young Man* is the Viking Press edition (1964), prepared by Chester G. Anderson, with Richard Ellmann: it is conveniently reprinted in *The Portable James Joyce*, edited by Harry Levin (Penguin, 1976), from which I quote p. 428.
2. Hugh Miller, *The Testimony of the Rocks: or, Geology in its Bearings on the Two Theologies, Natural and Revealed*. Boston, 1857, p. 277.
3. *The Portable James Joyce*, p. 429.
4. 'The Boarding House' in ibid., p. 71.
5. *Ulysses*. London: Bodley Head, 1947 reprint, p. 25.
6. Ibid., p. 101.
7. Fredric Jameson, *Fables of Aggression*. Berkeley and Los Angeles: University of California Press, 1979, p. 57.
8. Arthur Power, *Conversations with James Joyce*, edited by Clive Hart. London: Millington, 1974, p. 48.
9. E. A. Wallis Budge, *The Gods of the Egyptians: or, Studies in Egyptian Mythology*. London: Methuen, 1904.
10. Mark L. Troy, *Mummeries of Resurrection*. Uppsala: University of Uppsala Publications, 1976.
11. *Finnegans Wake*. London: Faber and Faber, 1975, reprint, p. 570.
12. *The Portable James Joyce*, p. 453.
13. William Empson, 'The Theme of *Ulysses*' in *The Kenyon Review*, Vol. XVIII, Winter 1956, pp. 26–52.
14. Hugh Kenner, *A Colder Eye*. New York: Knopf, 1983, pp. 230, 231.

8: Literary Autobiography in Twentieth-Century Ireland
1. Letter to Katharine Tynan, 12 December 1913. *The Letters of W. B. Yeats*, edited by Allan Wade. London: Rupert Hart-Davies, 1954, p. 586.
2. George Moore, *Hail and Farewell*, edited by Richard Cave. Gerrards Cross: Colin Smythe, 1976, p. 51. Henceforth H. & F.
3. W. B. Yeats, *Autobiographies*. London: Macmillan, 1955, p. 431.
4. Ibid., p. 405.
5. See Joseph Ronsley, *Yeats's Autobiography*. Cambridge: Harvard University Press, 1968, pp. 20–33, for the publishing history of Yeats's autobiographical prose works.
6. W. B. Yeats, *Autobiographies*, p. 11.
7. H. & F., p. 533.
8. W. B. Yeats, *Autobiographies*, p. 315.
9. Ibid., 380.
10. Ibid., 381.
11. Seán O'Casey, *Autobiography, Book 5: Rose and Crown*. London: Pan Books, 1973, p. 34.
12. Frank O'Connor, *An Only Child*. London: Macmillian, 1965.
13. Sean O'Faolain, *Vive Moi*. London: Rupert Hart-Davies, 1965, p. 150.
14. Ibid., p. 169.

168   THE GENIUS OF IRISH PROSE

15. Ibid., p. 270.
16. Ibid., p. 274.
17. Ibid., p. 277.

9: Prose Writing Translated from the Irish
1. In 'A View of the State of Ireland' in *The Works of Edmund Spenser,* to which
is prefixed some account of the life of Spenser, by the Reverend Henry John
Todd, M.A., a new edition. London: George Routledge and Sons, 1872, p. 526.
2. Ibid., p. 527.
3. Aodh de Blácam, *Gaelic Literature Surveyed.* Second revised edition, 1929, p.
365.
4. Stopford A. Brooke, *On the Need and Use of Getting Irish Literature into the
English Tongue.* London: Fisher Unwin, 1893, quoted by Alan Titley in 'Litríocht
na Gaeilge, Litríocht an Bhéarla agus Irish Literature', in *Scríobh 5,* Seán Ó
Mórdha a chuir in eagar. Baile Átha Cliath: An Clóchomhar, 1981, pp. 125–6.
5. Douglas Hyde, *Love Songs of Connacht.* London: Fisher Unwin; Dublin: Gill,
1893, p.v.
6. *The Love Songs of Connacht,* collected and translated by Douglas Hyde, with
a preface by W. B. Yeats. Dublin: Dun Emer Press, 1904. Quoted by Mícheál
Ó hAodha in his introduction to facsimile of 1893 volume; Shannon: Irish
University Press, 1969, p. vi.
7. Ernest Boyd, *Ireland's Literary Renaissance.* Dublin, 1916; reissued, Dublin:
Allen Figgis, 1968, p. 79.
8. Ibid., p. 72.
9. *Cuchulain of Muirtheimne,* the Story of the Men of the Red Branch of Ulster,
arranged and put into English by Lady Gregory, with a preface by W. B. Yeats.
London: John Murray, 1902; reissued, Gerrards Cross: Colin Smythe, 1970, p.
11.
10. Ibid., p. 11.
11. Edward Martyn, *The Dream Physician.* Dublin: Talbot Press. Quoted in
Sister Marie Thérèse Courtney, *Edward Martyn and the Irish Theatre.* New York:
Vantage Press, 1956, p. 140.
12. Joseph Hone, *The Life of George Moore,* London: Gollancz, 1936, p. 244.
13. E. R. Dodds, ed., *Journal and Letters of Stephen MacKenna.* London:
Constable, 1936, p. 218.
14. Quoted on the dust-jacket of *Each Actor on His Ass,* by Mícheál Mac
Liammóir. London: Routledge and Kegan Paul, 1961.
15. Introduction, Máirtín Ó Cadhain, *The Road to Brightcity,* translated from
the Irish by Eoghan Ó Tuairisc. Dublin: Poolbeg, 1981, p. 12.
16. Tomás Ó Criomhthain, *The Islandman,* translated by Robin Flower. Oxford:
University Press, 1951, p. 7.
17. Preface, Maurice O'Sullivan, *Twenty Years A-Growing,* rendered from the
original Irish by Moya Llewelyn Davies and George Thomson. London: Chatto
and Windus, 1933, p. 4.
18. Translator's note, *Peig, the Autobiography of Peig Sayers,* translated into
English by Bryan MacMahon. Dublin: Talbot Press, 1973, p. 7.
19. Quotation from the *Sunday Telegraph* on the dust-jacket of *An Irish Navvy,*
translated from the Irish of Donall Mac Amhlaigh by Valentin Iremonger.
London: Routledge and Kegan Paul, 1964.

10: Fable and Fantasy
1. Alan Denson, ed., *Letters from A. E.* London: Abelard-Schuman, 1961, p. 17.
2. W. B. Yeats, *Mythologies.* London: Macmillan, 1959, p. 281.

3. 'The Passing of the Shee', in *The Plays and Poems of J. M. Synge*, edited by T. R. Henn. London: Methuen, 1963, p. 295.
4. 'Bagpipe Music', in *The Collected Poems of Louis MacNeice*, edited by E. R. Dodds. London: Faber, p. 97.
5. C. S. Lewis, *On This and Other Worlds*. London: Collins, 1982, p. 152.
6. James Stephens, *The Crock of Gold*, London: Macmillan, 1912, p. 71.
7. Ibid., p. 311.
8. Eimar O'Duffy, *King Goshawk and the Birds*. London: Macmillan, 1926, p. 77.
9. Ibid., p. 83.
10. 'Canal Bank Walk', in *The Complete Poems of Patrick Kavanagh*, edited by Peter Kavanagh. New York: Peter Kavanagh Hand Press, 1972, p. 294.
11. Flann O'Brien, *The Third Policeman*. London: Hart–Davis/MacGibbon, 1967, p. 54.
12. Austin Clarke, *Collected Poems*. London: Allen and Unwin, 1936, p. 313.
13. Mervyn Wall, *The Unfortunate Fursey*. Dublin: Helicon, 1955, p. 233.
14. Ibid., pp. 233–4.
15. Mervyn Wall, *The Return of Fursey*. London: Pilot Press, 1948, pp. 82–3.
16. Robert Hogan, *Dictionary of Irish Literature*. Dublin: Gill and Macmillan, 1980, p. 412.

11: Samuel Beckett and the Protestant Ethic

1. Samuel Beckett, *Waiting for Godot*. London: Faber, 1965, p. 52.
2. Ibid., p. 13.
3. Owen Dudley Edwards, *James Connolly: The Mind of an Activist*. Dublin: 1971. See especially Chapter Three.
4. George Bernard Shaw, 'The Protestants of Ireland' (1912), in *The Matter with Ireland*, edited by David H. Greene and Dan H. Laurence. London: Hart–Davis, 1962, p. 73.
5. Deirdre Bair, *Samuel Beckett: A Biography*. London: Johathan Cape, 1978, p. 18.
6. See Hugh Kenner, *A Reader's Guide to Samuel Beckett*. London: Thames and Hudson, 1973, p. 49.
7. Samuel Beckett, *More Pricks Than Kicks*. London: Calder, 1970, p. 64.
8. Ibid., p. 64.
9. Ibid., p. 79.
10. Ibid., p. 21.
11. Samuel Beckett, *Murphy*. London: Picador, 1973, p. 36.
12. Ibid., p. 102.
13. Ibid., p. 42.
14. Ibid., p. 42.
15. Ibid., p. 50.
16. Ibid., p. 50.
17. Ibid., p. 50.
18. Ibid., p. 86.
19. Quoted by Kenner, *Reader's Guide*, pp. 52–3.
20. Quoted by Bair, *Samuel Beckett*, p. 198.
21. Quoted by Bair, ibid., p. 351.
22. Kenner, *Reader's Guide*, p. 134.
23. Quoted by Bair, *Samuel Beckett*, p. 352.
24. Samuel Beckett, *Molloy, Malone Dies, The Unnamable*. London: Calder, 1959, p. 108.
25. Ibid., p. 170.
26. Ibid., p. 129.

27. Ibid., p. 257.
28. Ibid., p. 246.
29. Ibid., p. 376.

12: The Short Story after the Second World War

1. The last collection from Liam O'Flaherty came as late as 1976, uncollected and unpublished pieces edited by A. A. Kelly, *The Pedlar's Revenge and Other Stories*. Dublin, Wolfhound Press. In 1982 Sean O'Faolain published six new stories written after *Foreign Affairs* (1976) in Volume Three of his *Collected Stories;* London: Constable. In 1981 there was a posthumous collection from Frank O'Connor (1903-66), *The Cornet Player who Betrayed Ireland*. Dublin: Poolbeg.
2. James Plunkett, *Collected Short Stories*. Dublin: Poolbeg, 1977, p. 31.
3. Ibid.
4. Ibid., p. 55.
5. Benedict Kiely, ed., *The Penguin Book of Irish Short Stories*. Harmondsworth: Penguin Books, 1981, p. 540.
6. Terence de Vere White, *Big Fleas and Little Fleas*. London: Victor Gollancz, 1976, p. 53.
7. Aidan Higgins, *Felo de Se*. London: John Calder, 1960, p. 62.
8. John Montague, *Death of a Chieftain*. London: Macgibbon and Kee, 1964, p. 142.
9. John McGahern, *Getting Through*. London: Faber, 1978, p. 1.
10. Kate Cruise O'Brien, *A Gift Horse*. Dublin: Poolbeg, 1978, p. 46.
11. Ibid.
12. Niall Quinn, *Voyavic*. Dublin: Wolfhound Press, 1980, p. 29.

13: The Realist Novel after the Second World War

1. *The Observer* London, 1 June 1966.
2. Benedict Kiely, *The Captain with the Whiskers*. London: Methuen, 1960, p. 46.
3. Francis MacManus, *Flow On Lovely River*. Dublin: Talbot Press, 1941, p. 26.
4. Francis MacManus, 'The Literature of the Period' in *The Years of the Great Test*. Cork: Mercier Press, 1962, p. 119.
5. John Cronin, 'Prose' in *Causeway – The arts in Northern Ireland,* Belfast: ACNI, 1971.
6. Sean O'Faolain (1949), 'The Dilemma in Irish Letters' in *The Month* II ,6, 1949, Dublin.

14: Literary Biography in Twentieth-Century Ireland

1. *Life of George Moore*. London: Victor Gollancz, 1936, p. 217.
2. Ibid., p. 231.
3. *W. B. Yeats, 1865-1939*. London: Macmillan, 1967, pp. 165-6.
4. Ibid., p. 197.
5. Ibid., p. 448.
6. *King of the Beggars*. New York: Viking Press, 1938, p. 105.
7. Ibid., p. 188.
8. Ibid., p. 265.
9. *The Road of Excess*. Dublin: Browne and Nolan, 1946, p. 67.
10. Ibid., p. 68.
11. Ibid., pp. 319-20.
12. *The Parents of Oscar Wilde*. London: Hodder and Stoughton, 1967, p. 196.

Bibliography:
Hone, Joseph, *Life of George Moore*. London: Victor Gollancz, 1936.
——, *W. B. Yeats, 1865-1939*. London: Macmillan, 1943, 1967.
O'Connor, Frank, *The Big Fellow. A Life of Michael Collins*. London: Nelson, 1937.
O'Connor, Ulick, *Brendan Behan*. London: Hamish Hamilton, 1970.
——, *The Times I've Seen: Oliver St John Gogarty*. New York: Astor-Honor, 1964.
O'Faolain, Sean, *The Life Story of Eamon de Valera*. Dublin: Talbot Press, 1932.
——, *Constance Markievicz, or The Average Revolutionary*. London: Jonathan Cape, 1934.
——, *King of the Beggars. A Life of Daniel O'Connell, the Irish Liberator, in a Study of the Rise of the Modern Irish Democracy (1775-1847)*. New York: Viking Press, 1938.
——, *De Valera*. Harmondsworth: Penguin, 1939.
——, *The Great O'Neill. A Biography of Hugh O'Neill, Earl of Tyrone, 1550-1616*. London: Longmans, Green and Co., 1942.
——, *Newman's Way. The Odyssey of John Henry Newman*. London: Longmans, Green and Co., 1952.
de Vere White, Terence, *The Road of Excess*. Dublin: Browne and Nolan, 1946.
——, *Kevin O'Higgins*. London: Methuen, 1948.
——, *The Parents of Oscar Wilde*. London: Hodder and Stoughton, 1967.

Select Bibliography

The individual books treated in the text are fully annotated in
the case of each individual chapter in the footnote references.
The books listed below provide a guide to further titles in the
various categories of Anglo-Irish prose.

Ernest A. Boyd, *Ireland's Literary Renaissance,* (1922).
Reissued; Dublin: Allen Figgis, 1968.

Stephen James Brown, *Ireland in Fiction. A Guide to Irish
Novels, Tales, Romances and Folklore.* Dublin: Maunsel,
1914.

James M. Cahalan, *Great Hatred, Little Room: The Irish
Historical Novel.* Dublin: Gill and Macmillan, 1984.

Peter Costello, *The Heart Grown Brutal. The Irish Revolution
in Literature from Parnell to the Death of Yeats.* Dublin: Gill
and Macmillan, 1977.

Allen, A. Eager, *A Guide to Irish Bibliographical Material.*
London: Library Association, 1980.

John Cronin, *The Anglo-Irish Novel.* Vol. 1, The Nineteenth
Century. Belfast; Appletree Press, 1980.

Aodh de Blacam, *Irish Literature Surveyed.* Dublin: Talbot
Press, 1933. Reissued; Talbot Press, 1973.

Richard Fallis, *The Irish Renaissance. An Introduction to Anglo-
Irish Literature.* Dublin: Gill and Macmillan, 1978.

Thomas Flanagan, *The Irish Novelists, 1900-1950.* New York;
Columbia University Press, 1959.

Maurice Harmon, *Anglo-Irish Literature and its Backgrounds. An
Irish Studies Handbook.* Dublin:Wolfhound Press, 1977.

Robert Hogan, gen. ed., *Dictionary of Irish Literature.* Dublin:
Gill and Macmillan, 1980.

Douglas Hyde, *The Literary History of Ireland.* London: T.
Fisher Unwin, 1899; new edition, with introduction by
Brian Ó Cuív; London: Ernest Benn, 1967.

A. Norman Jeffares, *Anglo-Irish Literature.* London:
Macmillan, 1982.

Benedict Kiely, *Modern Irish Fiction. A Critique.* Dublin:
Golden Eagle Books, 1950.

Francis MacManus, ed., *The Years of the Great Test, 1926-1939*. Thomas Davis Lectures. Cork: Mercier Press, 1967.

Roger McHugh and Maurice Harmon, *Anglo-Irish Literature. From its Origins to the Present Day*. Dublin: Wolfhound Press, 1982.

Augustine Martin, *Anglo-Irish Literature*. Dublin: Department of Foreign Affairs, 1980.

Vivian Mercier, *The Irish Comic Tradition*. Oxford; Clarendon Press, 1962.

Kevin B. Nowlan and T. Desmond Williams, eds, *Ireland in the War Years and After, 1939-1951*. Thomas Davis Lectures. Dublin: Gill and Macmillan, 1969.

Frank O'Connor, *The Lonely Voice. Studies in the Short Story*. London: Macmillan, 1963.

———, *The Backward Look. Irish Literary History*. London: Macmillan, 1967.

Patrick Rafroidi and Maurice Harmon, eds, *The Irish Novel in Our Time*. Lille: Lille University Press, 1976.

Patrick Rafroidi and Terence Brown, eds, *The Irish Short Story. Studies of Irish Writers and their Work*. Gerrards Cross, Colin Smythe, 1979.

The Contributors

John Cronin, author of *The Anglo Irish Novel,* Professor of English, Queen's University, Belfast.

Richard Allen Cave, scholar and critic, Senior Lecturer in English at Bedford College, London University.

Colbert Kearney, critic and biographer, Statutory Lecturer, University College, Cork.

A. Norman Jeffares, scholar and critic, Professor of English, University of Stirling.

Benedict Kiely, novelist, short story writer, author of *Modern Irish Fiction: A Critique.*

Thomas Kilroy, playwright and novelist, Professor of English, University College, Galway.

Denis Donoghue, literary critic and theorist, Henry James Professor of Letters, New York University.

Terence Brown, critic and literary historian, Professor in English, Trinity College, Dublin.

Proinsias Ó Conluain, broadcaster and critic of Irish Literature.

Augustine Martin, Professor of Anglo-Irish Literature and Drama, University College, Dublin.

Declan Kiberd, critic in English and Irish literature, Lecturer in Anglo-Irish Literature, University College, Dublin.

John Jordan, short story writer, critic and broadcaster.

Seán McMahon, teacher, critic and literary editor.

Maurice Harmon, critic, editor of *The Irish University Review,* Associate Professor of Anglo-Irish Literature, University College, Dublin.

Communications and Community in Ireland

Edited by Brian Farrell

To mark World Communications Year 1983 Radio Telefís Éireann broadcast a series of ten Thomas Davis Lectures dealing with the role of communication in the evolution of the modern community in Ireland.

These lectures now published in book form afford the reader the opportunity of seeing highlighted some of the major phases, incidents and personalities in the history of the media in Ireland. The series also links the Irish experience to comparable developments elsewhere and uses individual local cases to illustrate some general themes of modern mass communication studies.

Ireland and Australia

Edited by Colm Kiernan

Ireland and Australia is a series of six lectures which were broadcast on Radio Telefís Éireann between August and October 1983. The intention is to have something in print by 1988, when the Australian bicentenary will be celebrated, so that the Irish contribution to Australian history will not be overlooked. The first lecture deals with the beginnings of settlement in Australia, when one third of the convicts transported were Irish. Lt. Colonel Con Costello argues that the Irish convicts sent to Australia were different from their British equivalents in several respects. In particular, most of them came from country regions whereas in industrialised England they mostly came from the cities. Dr David Fitzpatrick's lecture concentrates attention on the emigration of free Irishmen and women to Australia during the nineteenth century, proposing that they were very successful in coming to terms with the opportunities that existed in the newly-settled continent. Professor Geoffrey Bolton concentrated his attention on the massive immigration movement that followed the discovery of gold in Australia. The population of Australia doubled in less than ten years and the foundations were set of modern Australia.

Karl Marx:
The Materialist Messiah

Edited by **Kevin B. Nowlan**

Karl Marx died in London on 14 March 1883. To commemorate the centenary of his death, Radio Telefís Éireann transmitted the lectures published in this volume as a part of the Thomas Davis Lecture Series. In these talks, a number of scholars, working in Ireland, have attempted to assess Marx's contribution to the shaping of the modern world. In devising these lectures an attempt was made to provide a chronological structure in the earlier lectures and to include a number of more specialised studies. The approaches of the individual contributors to Marx and the Marxist tradition vary, but all are concerned to present a balanced discussion which should help the reader to see Marx and his colleague, Friedrich Engels, in a fair perspective. In two of the lectures the contributors have considered the fascinating question of Marx, Engels and Ireland and the influence of Marxist ideas on Irish revolutionary thought and action in the opening decades of this century.

No neat, dogmatic image of Marx emerges from these lectures and this is not surprising, given the range of his writings, the difficulties of interpretation and the various groups and parties, which have emerged over the last hundred years, all claiming to be the true exponents of the prophet's teachings. The glosses on his words and the attempts to apply his theories and projections to a changing world have tended to distract attention from what Marx and Engels said in their time and in the context of their own experiences.